THE WAYS OF THE
SAMURAI

THE WAYS OF THE SAMURAI

From Ronins to Ninjas
the Fiercest Warriors in Japanese History

CAROL GASKIN & VINCE HAWKINS

FALL
RIVER
PRESS

Fall River Press
122 Fifth Avenue
New York, NY 10011

ISBN-13: 978-0-7607-7047-4
ISBN-10: 0-7607-7047-6

Printed and bound in the United States of America

5   7   9   11   13   15   14   12   10   8   6   4

CONTENTS

The armor of the samurai

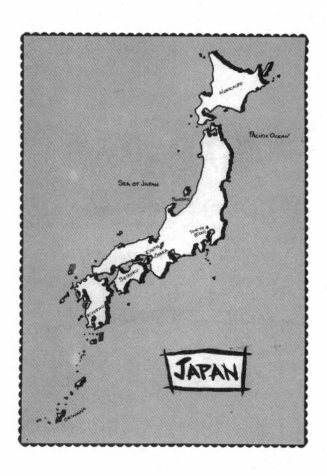

HOKKAIDO

PACIFIC OCEAN

SEA OF JAPAN

HONSHU

TOKYO
(EDO)

KYOTO
OSAKA

SHIKOKU

KYUSHU

OKINAWA

JAPAN

1

THE FIRST SAMURAI

The field was lit by ghostly torches. Calm yet alert, the men waited for dawn. They were ready for war, dressed in family colors, their metal armor laced together with cords of brilliant hues. Their weapons were at their sides. Their battle flags, bearing the crest of their lord and leader, flapped in the wind. The horses were still.

Suddenly, at the break of dawn, the horses stirred. The men were instantly alert. And their leader, resplendent in fine armor and patterned silks, rose to his feet. His face was hidden by a ferocious iron mask, and his helmet bore the

1

golden horns of a crescent moon. For a moment, he stood as still as a statue, listening and studying the horizon. He sniffed at the air and eyed the horses. Then the great warlord let out a fierce battle cry. The men hurried to their stations.

As the rising sun washed the field with a pale orange glow, the enemy thundered into view—hundreds of archers on horseback, screaming fearsome war cries.

The mounted archers faced one other in two noisy battle lines. At once, the air above the battlefield was crisscrossed with whistling volleys of arrows. Wounded horses fell to the ground, whinnying in pain. Wounded warriors would pull the arrows from their limbs and continue to fight as long as they were able.

All at once the battlefield quieted as a lone figure galloped forward. His armor bore the crest of the enemy, and his helmet was decorated with great antlers. He reined in his horse and shouted his name and the names of his family. "I am a warrior worth one thousand men. Is there a worthy man who dares come forth to combat me?"

Rising to the challenge, the warlord rode

forth. The crescent horns on his helmet shone like fire in the new morning. "My ancestors are each worth *ten* thousand men. Our honor is famed throughout the land!"

The two warriors charged each another at full gallop, each daring the other to pull away first. But neither would be proved a coward. Driven to a frenzy, their horses collided with a bone-breaking crash, and the warriors tumbled to the ground.

In a flash, their swords were drawn. The glinting metal whipped through the air as the men circled each other in a deadly dance. Sparks flew from clashing steel. Seeing an opening, the challenger thrust his sword at the warlord's neck. The warlord moved swiftly aside. *"Eeeeiiiii!"* he cried, sweeping his sword before him. Slowly, the warrior with the antlered helmet crumpled and fell to the ground, mortally wounded. Leaning over his foe, the warrior of the crescent moon made a final swipe with his sword and with a cry of triumph held aloft his enemy's head.

Spurred on by his victory, the warlord's men charged, and the enemy attackers made a hasty retreat. The battle was over. The warriors were satisfied. The enemy warlord had been a worthy foe and had died an honorable death. But who were these fierce swordsmen? By what strange rules did they fight?

The warriors were *samurai*, professional soldiers who served the rival warlords of Japan. Tales of the samurai and their famous code of honor have fascinated generations.

But the earliest samurai were not known for their swordsmanship. Their way was called The Way of the Bow and the Horse.

THE WAY OF THE BOW AND THE HORSE

Japan is a group of beautiful, mountainous islands in the Pacific Ocean, off the coast of eastern Asia. It is separated from Russia, China, and Korea by the Sea of Japan.

In early times, Japan was ruled by an emperor and his court. The emperor was treated like a god and was believed to be descended from the sun goddess, *Amateratsu*. Beneath the emperor in rank were the noblemen and below the noblemen were many ranks of samurai. Lower in rank were the peasant farmers who worked the lands of the noblemen. At this time, anyone could rise to become a samurai. But in later Japan, only those born to samurai parents could hold the rank of samurai.

The word *samurai* means "to serve." Originally, the samurai were soldiers who served the imperial court and were absolutely loyal to the emperor. But they also protected the families of noblemen.

Since earliest times, Japan's principal crop has been rice. Whoever owned the rice fields controlled the wealth of the country. By the 12th century, many powerful noblemen owned lands and castles far from the emperor's palace in Kyoto. To protect themselves from bands of thieves—and from one another—the noblemen began to keep their own private armies of samurai. The favored weapons were the bow and arrow and the spear.

A samurai warrior followed a code of honor called *bushido*—"the Way of the Warrior." He promised complete loyalty to his lord. An individual samurai could distinguish himself in battle and be granted his own lands.

With the support of their samurai armies, the noblemen gained control of vast territories.

These noble families then joined together to form clans that in turn grew to be more powerful than the emperor himself. The clans were often at war with one another.

Finally, civil war broke out between the two most powerful clans: the Minamoto, or Genji, and the Taira, or Heike. And Japan entered the Age of the Sword.

A SAMURAI'S GREATEST TREASURE: THE SAMURAI SWORD

In all of the ancient tales of our world's beginnings, the first sword ever recorded was a Japanese blade called the "Cloud Cluster Sword." This mighty blade was forged in the tail of a gigantic eight-headed serpent, whose lower body was hidden by smoky black clouds.

The serpent, who was as large as eight mountains, liked to eat young maidens. So the hero Susano-o, son of the fire god, set out to slay the monster. He tricked the serpent into drinking too much *sake*, a strong rice wine. The drunken serpent soon slept, and Susano-o cut him to pieces. But when he reached the serpent's tail, Susano-o's sword struck something very hard and broke in two. Reaching into the dark clouds, he discovered the Cloud Cluster Sword. According to legend, the sword was one of three treasures that were handed down by the gods to the first emperor of Japan to form the Japanese Royal Regalia, or crown jewels. (An iron mirror and a jeweled necklace were the other two.) Thus the sword, a symbol of the emperor's divine power, has been sacred to the Japanese since earliest times.

Tokugawa Ieyasu (1542-1616), one of the greatest samurai warlords, called the sword "the soul of the samurai." During Ieyasu's time, only a samurai was allowed the privilege of wearing two swords. The longer sword, the *katana*, was his primary battle weapon. The shorter sword, the *wakizashi*, was also used for fighting, and, if necessary, for ritual suicide.

To a proud samurai, no possession was more precious than his sword. A sword was brought to the birthing chamber when a samurai was born and placed by his deathbed when he died. During his lifetime, a samurai slept with his sword next to his pillow, and he carried it with him wherever he went.

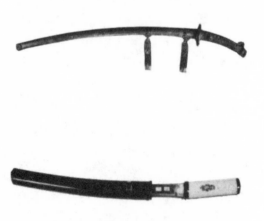

Top: The katana, the long sword.
Bottom: The wakizashi, the short sword.

Swords were always treated with respect. When visiting another warrior, a samurai might place his katana in a special rack near the door or allow a servant to carry it in a silken cloth, but he kept his wakizashi by his side.

Samurai swords were handed down for generations. Any disrespect to a samurai's weapon was seen as an insult to his entire family. It was considered a grave offense to touch another's sword in any way without permission—an affront that could result in a bloody duel. So samurai had to be very careful not to bump into one another while walking in the street.

Samurai also believed that the finest blades by the best sword makers had spiritual powers of their own. Swords that had performed in battle were especially valued. But wealthy samurai also sought new swords by famous sword makers.

Sword makers were revered as artists and holy men, and a sword maker's shop was seen as a shrine, where holy work was done. A typical sign outside such a shop might read: "Souls polished here."

The personality of a sword maker was thought to enter his blades. So before forging a sword, a master sword maker would fast to purify himself. He would hang prayers written on rice paper about his shop and would dress in white robes, like a priest, to work at the fiery forge. While he worked he would concentrate deeply.

A samurai sword was made of iron and steel, alternately heated in the forge and cooled, or tempered, in a mixture of oil and water. The steel was hammered, folded over, and hammered again, to make up to four million layers of metal. The cutting edge of a samurai sword was very hard and extremely sharp, but the body of the blade was softer and more flexible. When it

A sword maker's workshop.

was finished, a sword would be decorated, and an ornate handle added. Then the new sword might be tested on the corpse of a criminal.

Like an artist, a master sword maker would often sign his work. But the most famous of all sword makers, Masamune (1264-1343), forged blades that were so distinctive he did not need to sign them. Masamune was known as a deeply religious man, and his swords were said to possess great spiritual power.

Masamune's chief rival, Muramasa, was also a skilled swordsmith. But Muramasa loved war. His blades were so strong they could slice an iron helmet like a melon. His swords had a thirst for blood. Samurai who owned Muramasa's evil swords were said to be driven mad, unable to stop killing, until finally they would turn the swords on themselves.

According to legend, one way to test the difference in character between Masamune's blades and Muramasa's is to stand one of each upright in a running stream. Leaves drifting in the water will avoid the sword by Masamune, passing safely to either side. But they will be drawn as if by a magnet to the deadly blade of Muramasa and be sliced in two.

Minamoto Yoritomo, the first shogun.

2

WAR BETWEEN WARLORDS

THE FIRST SHOGUN

The Gempei War between the Minamoto and the Taira clans began in 1180 and lasted for five years. Stories of this fierce civil war and the heroes who fought in it have become legends in Japan. For 800 years, the Japanese have repeated the stories in books, plays, and films—much as Americans retell the legends of the revolutionary war and the wild west.

The Minamoto clansmen were the winners of the Gempei War. Their leader, Minamoto Yoritomo, became the first *shogun,* or military dictator, of Japan. For centuries thereafter, the emperor of Japan ruled in name only. The real power belonged to the shogun.

Minamoto Yoritomo was a great statesman but a cold leader. Today, it is Yoritomo's brother, Minamoto Yoshitsune, who is remembered as the perfect samurai warrior.

A note about Japanese names: In Japan, it is customary for the surname, or family name, to go first, followed by the given name. *Minamoto,* for example, is a family name—like *Smith,* while *Yoritomo* is a given name. Often, given names in a Japanese family begin with the same sound, like Yori or Yoshi. A comparable example in English would be a family of Smiths who named their children "Smith Joanne," "Smith Joseph," and "Smith Jody."

WAR BETWEEN WARLORDS

The emperor's power had been greatly weakened

by the rise of the samurai clans. The two most powerful, the Minamoto and the Taira, had long been rivals. The Minamoto were known for quelling rebellions in the north and east, while the Taira were expert at defeating the pirates who plagued the trade routes to China. The Taira flew a flag of red. The Minamoto color was white.

In 1160, the Minamoto clan attacked the Imperial Palace in Kyoto. They were defeated by Kiyomori, leader of the Taira, who seized control of the capital.

Kiyomori ordered the execution of the Minamoto leader, Yoshitomo, and all of his sons. Yoshitomo was murdered. But Kiyomori was struck by the beauty of Yoshitomo's wife, Tokiwa. He agreed to let her children live if she would become his mistress. So the oldest son, Yoritomo, a 14-year-old who had fought at his father's side, was sent to be raised by Taira in the eastern province of Izu. The youngest son, Yoshitsune, still a baby, was sent to a monastery to be trained as a priest.

Taira Kiyomori was later to be sorry. For the boys whose lives he had spared would one day return to take their revenge.

TALES OF YOSHITSUNE

As he grew to manhood, Minamoto Yoritomo studied politics and warfare under the watchful eyes of his sworn enemies, the Taira. The childhood of his brother Yoshitsune, however, was quite different. Today Yoshitsune's story is part history, part legend.

As an infant, Yoshitsune was sent to a remote temple on Mount Kurama. At the age of eleven, learning of his true heritage, it is said he resolved to conquer the Taira and secretly began to study the martial arts. Legend tells us Yoshitsune would sneak out of the monastery at night, to be tutored by Sojobo, king of the *tengu*. The tengu, small mountain goblins who were half bird and half men, used magic to teach the boy swordsmanship, archery, and other skills. As soon as Yoshitsune would strike with a sword, his teacher would vanish, only to reappear laughing at the top of a tree. The boy would let an arrow fly, but the tengu would knock it back to earth with an iron fan. One tengu would appear in front of him, while another attacked from behind. Training night after night, Yoshitsune gradually became a warrior of uncanny awareness, speed, and skill.

There are many tales of Yoshitsune's adventures after he stole away from the monks at Mount Kurama. Most popular is the story of his meeting with the huge warrior who would become his lifelong companion—Benkei.

Benkei was a warrior monk. He was a ferocious fighter with the *naginata,* a spear with a curved blade, the traditional weapon of Japanese monks. He was also a giant. Benkei's hobby was collecting swords. Every day he would wait on the Gojo Bridge for warriors who wanted to cross. He would challenge them to fight and "collect" their swords. He had 999 already, and he wanted 1,000.

One day, Benkei spotted a graceful lad with a beautiful sword. The youth was seated under a tree on the far side of the bridge, quietly playing the flute. Benkei was disappointed that his 1,000th sword would be so easy to take—like taking candy from a baby. But he wanted to finish his collection.

"Give me your sword," demanded Benkei. "Just put it down on the ground and be off." Much to his surprise, the young man ignored him.

"Do as I say, or I'll have to bash in your

head," growled the giant. But the sweet tones of the flute continued.

Benkei swung his naginata. But to his amazement, he struck the ground beneath the tree. The youth had leaped onto the railing of the bridge, where he balanced calmly.

Benkei swung again, and again the lad avoided his blow. It was as though he had flown to the opposite railing of the bridge! Faster and faster, harder and harder Benkei swung, only to strike thin air. Soon the giant was exhausted and paused to get his breath. Appearing not the slightest bit tired, the young man whipped a small fan from the folds of his garment. He fanned himself for a moment, as though bored with the fight. Then, with a flick of his wrist, he loosed the fan through the air, striking the giant squarely on the head.

From that day forth, Benkei called the young man his master. The young man was, of course, Yoshitsune.

THE GEMPEI WAR

In 1180, Kiyomori's three-year-old grandson, Antoku, became emperor—and Taira Kiyomori

effectively ruled Japan. He had long since forgotten about the Minamoto heirs he had ban-
ished 20 years earlier. So he was very surprised
to hear that the Minamoto were planning an
uprising against the Taira clan.

The first strike was a disaster for the Minamoto. Their small force was led by a 74-year-
old veteran warrior, Minamoto Yorimasa, and
was made up of his loyal retainers and a band
of warrior monks. Their plot discovered early,
the Minamoto forces found themselves trapped
in a town called Uji on the banks of the Uji
River, on the road between Kyoto and Nara.
Pursued by the Taira and greatly outnumbered,
the Minamoto hit upon a plan. They crossed the
Uji Bridge, and removed some 60 feet of the
wooden planking. At dawn, shrouded in mist,
the Taira samurai galloped to the river's edge
and raised their war cry. The Minamoto
answered. So the Taira horsemen thundered
across the bridge and tumbled through the hole
into the swiftly flowing river.

The sky above the river was soon thick with
arrows, and many a brave duel was fought on
the broken bridge. But the Minamoto luck did
not hold out. Joining hands and lowering their
heads against the Minamoto bowmen, the Taira

The Battle at Uji Bridge

forces forded the river and attacked. Minamoto Yorimasa, wounded and defeated, composed a farewell poem on the back of his war fan. Then, cutting across his abdomen with his dagger, he committed suicide by *seppuku* and had his head sunk in the river so no enemy could claim it. For centuries, Yorimasa was remembered as a model of composure and nobility in defeat—a most honorable samurai death.

The war raged on. The Minamoto forces were decimated, and the Taira appeared to be winning. But Minamoto Yoritomo, now come of age, always escaped. On his deathbed in 1181,

Taira Kiyomori commanded his men not to pray for him, but only to bring him the head of Yoritomo and place it on his tomb.

Yoritomo had made his headquarters at Kamakura. There, he was reunited with his young brother Yoshitsune. Yoritomo's power grew, and he began to call himself Lord Kamakura. But he soon found he had a rival in his own family. His cousin Minamoto Yoshinaka was making great inroads against the Taira. In 1183, the Taira fled the capital city, retreating to their territory in western Honshu and to the islands of Shikoku and Kyushu. They took with them the imperial regalia—the mirror, the jeweled necklace, and the sword—the child Emperor Antoku, not yet six years old, and most of the royal family. Yoshinaka entered Kyoto in triumph.

But Yoshinaka was a rough country soldier, and his samurai ravaged Kyoto. In 1184, Yoritomo sent Yoshitsune to conquer their cousin. Yoshinaka had the planking torn up on the Uji Bridge, hoping the trick would work again. But Yoshitsune's men forded the river upstream and took the capital. Yoshinaka was beheaded.

With Kyoto secured, the Minamoto wanted

to put an end to the Taira clan once and for all. Yoshitsune led many brilliant attacks, crushing Taira strongholds and torching Taira camps. The Taira were powerful and controlled the waters of the Inland Sea. But as their losses mounted, some of the seafaring samurai warlords joined the Minamoto.

DAN-NO-URA

In 1185, the Taira gathered all their ships together in a narrow strait between the islands of Kyushu and Honshu, near the village of Dan-no-ura. With their superior experience at sea warfare, learned from generations of fighting pirates, the Taira were confident they would quickly crush the Minamoto ships. They were sure the battle would be so short it would be over before high tide.

At first, the Taira seemed to be winning. A Taira general fought his way onto Yoshitsune's boat and came close to capturing the hero. But Yoshitsune made a spectacular leap to an adjoining ship, and the Taira general jumped to his death in the sea. The battle raged on. And. the tide began to rise.

The Taira ships were trapped between the

Minamoto ships and the shore when the tide turned. All at once the Taira were being forced toward the shore. Yoshitsune commanded his men to direct their arrows at the enemy helmsmen rather than at the archers on deck. Soon the Taira ships were floundering in the current, helplessly out of control. The seas ran red with blood. Finally, one of the Taira captains lowered the red Taira flag and sailed off to join the Minamoto. The captain told Yoshitsune which of the Taira ships held the boy emperor and the crown jewels.

Yoshitsune directed the full force of his warriors against that single ship.

Tomomori, the Taira warlord, knew that all was lost. He informed the young emperor that suicide was the only honorable answer. The child's grandmother, the widow of Kiyomori, then took the eight-year-old emperor in her arms, led him in a final prayer, and leapt with him into the churning sea.

Tragedy followed. Next to jump were other members of the imperial family and many Taira samurai. As one of the royal women was about to jump, an arrow pinned her skirt to the side of the ship and she dropped the casket she was holding onto the deck of the ship. Minamoto warriors rescued the casket. Inside, they found the sacred mirror, one of the imperial regalia. Later, Yoshitsune's divers recovered the jewel from the bottom of the sea. But the legendary Cloud Cluster Sword was lost forever.

Last to jump was Tomomori, the Taira general, who put on two suits of heavy armor and followed his men into the churning water.

As head of the victorious Minamoto clan, Yoritomo became shogun of Japan. But for years, sailors avoided the coast of Dan-no-ura, where ghostly armies were reported to haunt the seas. Tales of the noble Taira, or Heike, are still told to this day. And the spirits of the samurai who were slain at Dan-no-ura are said to live on in the Heike crabs, which bear the imprints of human faces on their shell.

Yoshitsune was a hero and had shown great loyalty to his brother and his clan. But Yoritomo was a politician, not a general. He was threatened by Yoshitsune's popularity and strength. His jealousy of his younger brother was so strong that he ordered Yoshitsune killed and had him hunted like an animal.

Yoshitsune wrote letters to Yoritomo swearing

his loyalty and pleading to be forgiven, but to no avail. With his faithful Benkei, he is said to have escaped his brother's armies and spies, met with ghosts, and had innumerable adventures. But at last he was trapped by the shogun's armies. While Benkei stood guard, fiercely bearing his naginata, Yoshitsune retired in private to commit suicide. Only when a mounted samurai dared to ride close to the ferocious Benkei did the warriors realize that he, too, was already dead. The giant simply fell over.

Yoritomo continued to rule alone. But some say he was tormented by guilt over the way he had treated his brother. In 1199, while riding in a procession, he was suddenly thrown from his horse to his death—for no apparent reason. Legend has it he was frightened to death by the ghost of Yoshitsune.

Osaka Castle, built in 1583 by Hideyoshi.

3

THE HEIGHT OF THE SAMURAI

THE MONGOL INVASIONS

One Japanese legend claims that Yoshitsune did not die in 1189 after all, but that he escaped to China where he joined the Mongols, changing his name to Genghis Khan.

Genghis Khan was one of the greatest conquerors in history. He united the Mongol tribes of China, and at his death he ruled an empire that stretched from Asia to eastern Europe. His grandson, Kublai Khan, tried to invade Japan and nearly succeeded.

The first Mongol invasion came in 1274. It was a severe trial for the samurai warriors, who found that their enemies had no interest in their traditional ways of warfare. Rather than making an honorable challenge to an equal opponent, the Mongol warriors slaughtered innocent women and children. But the samurai fought bravely, and the Mongols retreated.

The second Mongol invasion came in 1281. This time, the Mongol fleet was enormous. While the samurai fought off a Mongol onslaught on the beaches, an imperial envoy was sent to pray to the sun goddess for divine help. That night, the skies grew dark and a whirling tornado began to blow. The waves rose high and fell crashing to the sea. The Mongol ships were tossed on the waves like toys. Then, powerful winds drove them onto the rocks, smashing them to splinters. The storm was called the *kamikaze,* or "divine winds."

Six centuries passed before any foreigner dared try to conquer Japan again. But the country remained torn by war from within. The wars became so numerous that the period from 1467 to 1568 is called the Age of War.

THE AGE OF WAR

By the mid-1400s, Japan was made up of many small states. Each of these states was ruled by a *daimyo,* a powerful landowner who controlled his territory from a fortified castle. Serving each daimyo was his personal samurai army, as well as troops of peasants known as *ashigaru,* meaning "light feet."

The daimyo were constantly at war with one another. By the mid-1500s, the emperor had neither power nor money, and the office of shogun had become meaningless. No single daimyo was powerful enough to unite Japan.

Then, in 1543, Japan was again visited by foreigners. This time it was the Portuguese, who brought something new with them: guns—the first firearms the Japanese had ever seen. The Portuguese had not come to conquer Japan, but to trade. One powerful lord gave his swordsmith a gun to copy. The swordsmith was puzzled. But rather than disappoint his lord, he traded his daughter for a series of lessons in gunsmithery.

This painting shows long-nosed Portugese monks worshipping at the shrine of their Christian God.

Soon the Japanese were making guns of their own.

One bold samurai, Oda Nobunaga, began his career as a minor warlord. But he was wise enough to recognize the value of firearms in warfare. By the time of his murder in 1583—by bullet wound—he had taken control of most of Japan. (For more see "The Battle of Nagashino: June 29, 1575.")

Nobunaga was succeeded by one of his generals, Toyotomi Hideyoshi. Hideyoshi was a small man who is said to have looked like a monkey. But on the battlefield he looked like a god. His magnificent helmet was decorated with a sunburst crest that surrounded his head like the rays of the sun. In only ten years, Hideyoshi managed to unite all of Japan. Before his death, he had become so confident of his abilities as a conqueror, that he invaded Korea—without success. Some say he had been possessed by a fox—a polite way of saying he was crazy. But his power could not be denied.

In 1586, Hideyoshi finished building Osaka Castle, one of the largest buildings in the world at that time. The walls were decorated with the finest paintings, and entire rooms were filled with silver and gold. All the riches in the world could not buy Hideyoshi his last wish, however. On his deathbed in 1598, he begged his generals to swear their loyalty to his only son and heir, Hideyori. Then, as if he knew that nothing could last forever, Hideyoshi composed a farewell poem:

Ah! As the dew I fall,
As the dew I vanish.
Even Osaka fortress
Is a dream within a dream.

Hideyori, the new ruler, was only five years old.

Soon after Hideyoshi's death, only half of his followers continued to support young Hideyori. The others joined forces with Hideyoshi's most trusted general, Tokugawa Ieyasu.

Ieyasu was brilliant and ambitious. He had fought his first battle as a young samurai of 17. Now an experienced general in his fifties, he was ready to lead Japan. But Ieyasu was, above all, patient. In 1600, he defeated the supporters of Hideyori in the largest battle ever fought between samurai, the Battle of Sekigahara. It was a triumph. But still Ieyasu did not try to remove Hideyori from Osaka Castle. Rather, in 1603, he went to the emperor of Japan and claimed the title of shogun. Then, he set up rule from the city of Edo (now Tokyo).

As military dictator, Ieyasu had a wall built around the Imperial Palace in Kyoto. Its purpose, he said, was to protect the emperor and the 300 noble families who lived inside. There, among peaceful gardens and great riches, the courtiers could read, write, paint, and study, as if in a dream world. But no one was allowed to leave without the permission of Ieyasu. Thus, no one could effectively conspire against him.

Tokugawa Ieyasu made many other changes during his reign as shogun. His government was well organized, and his rules were rigid. He effectively halted the manufacture of guns and encouraged a return to the sword as the only weapon of honor. (For more, see "A Return to Traditional Ways.") He strictly controlled foreign trade, lest any one lord grow too powerful. Under his successors, foreigners were banned from Japan entirely, until trade was finally reopened in 1854.

Under Ieyasu, social classes were sharply divided. The government decided what each class could wear and how they could behave. Samurai were the ruling class. Beneath them were the farmers, the artisans, and finally the merchants.

Samurai were not always rich. Their wealth was dependent on the amount of land they controlled. But they were feared and respected.

Tokugawa Ieyasu

Only the sons of samurai were permitted to become samurai, and only samurai were allowed to wear two swords. A samurai had the authority to kill or spare anyone beneath him, for any reason. But along with their power came responsibility. A samurai would be harshly punished, even ordered to commit suicide, if disgraced.

Ieyasu, who fought in some 80 battles in his

lifetime, also encouraged his warriors to appreciate the finer things: poetry, the tea ceremony, the rising of the moon, the perfume of the cherry blossoms. A true samurai was a man of refined tastes.

In 1614, after ruling for 14 years, Ieyasu was ready to challenge Hideyori. He besieged Osaka Castle in one of the most famous of Japan's military campaigns, one of the last samurai battles in history. In this too, Ieyasu was successful, and Hideyori, trapped in the golden tower his father had built, committed suicide. Then, Ieyasu had Hideyori's son and many of his samurai decapitated to avoid any future rebellion.

Two years after his final victory, at the age of 74, Ieyasu died. A true samurai to the last, he brandished a sword on his deathbed. After his death, he was named a god: Toshogu, the Sun God of the East.

Ieyasu did not suffer the same misfortune of his predecessor, Hideyoshi. He ensured the peaceful succession of his son—a capable general in his own right—and the Tokugawa family ruled as shoguns for more than 250 years.

CAROL GASKIN AND VINCE HAWKINS

A JAPANESE CASTLE

Japanese castles were large enough to house the daimyo, his family, and his entire samurai army. They were usually built on a hill, either natural or man-made. The foundations were made of rock and formed steep, jagged walls. These helped to protect the castles from earthquakes, but they were also easy to climb. To prevent attackers from scaling the walls, the war lords built secret holes and trap doors through which boiling water could be poured and chutes through which tons of rock could be dropped. Inside the walls, there was often a moat or additional levels of walls that led to the main castle building—the keep.

The castle keep was built of wood but was generally safe from fire, because it was so hard to reach. The keep was many stories high, with huge, curving roofs as graceful as bird's wings, tiled in white or blue. Hidden among the windows and walls were openings for arrows and guns.

Inside, the Japanese castle was a maze of courtyards, rooms, and passages, cleverly constructed so an invader could be trapped in each section by a complicated system of gates.

At the center of the fortress were luxurious

apartments where the lords lived with their wives and children. Other floors held throne rooms, offices, storerooms, and living quarters for the soldiers and the servants.

Japanese castles were built to withstand attack. Some were burned, but many others stood until they were destroyed by the bombs of World War II. Today, only a few remain.

THE SIEGE OF OSAKA CASTLE, 1614

Besieging a Japanese castle was a long and costly affair. The attacks were usually savage and bloody. Surprise attacks were difficult to engineer, because the castles often had tower lookouts, so warriors had to haul huge scaling ladders to the outer walls or try to tunnel beneath them. Sometimes the best plan was simply to block supplies and starve the enemy out.

The Siege of Osaka Castle lasted nearly a year. The castle had a five-story keep, three moats, and rivers on three sides. It was defended by 120,000 men loyal to Hideyori, who would have liked nothing better than to display the head of

Tokugawa Ieyasu.

Ieyasu's first order of business was to capture the castle outposts. Then he built siege towers and ram parts and bombarded the castle for three days, while his miners tried to tunnel beneath the outer towers.

But nothing worked. The castle was well stocked, and it was the dead of winter.

Ieyasu knew he would have to resort to trickery. He bribed a traitor to open the castle gates. But the man was beheaded before he even got close. So Ieyasu turned his largest cannons on the ladies' quarters, where Hideyori's mother, Yodogimi, lived.

The ladies were unable to sleep at all. One cannon ball smashed Yodigimi's tea cabinet, killing two of her servants, while 100,000 samurai yelled and screamed from the ramparts they had built outside Yodogimi's quarters.

Hideyori, pressured by his mother and fearful that the castle had been weakened, agreed to peace terms, Ieyasu would disband his army and guarantee Hideyori's safety on the condition that Hideyori agree not to attack him, and incidentally, that the outer moat of the castle be filled in.

Ieyasu's troops capture Osaka Castle

Ieyasu pretended to disband his forces and ordered them, on their way out, to dismantle the outer wall of Osaka Castle and use it to fill in the outer moat. Then, while the Osaka commanders objected, they began to fill in the second moat! Ieyasu pretended that they must have misunderstood his orders. But the defenses of Osaka Castle had been reduced to a single moat and wall.

The following summer, Hideyori's men came after Ieyasu. But their attack backfired, and this time Ieyasu's battle strategy and siege craft worked. Osaka Castle went up in flames. Trapped inside, Hideyori and Yodogimi commited suicide.

The ronin.

4

TALES OF THE RONIN

THE RONIN

Under the Tokugawa shoguns, many of the lesser daimyo were exiled, and their armies disbanded, leaving a large class of masterless samurai. They were called *ronin*, which means "wave man"—one who is tossed here and there, as if on the waves of the sea.

The ronin had neither clan nor lord and were often treated as outcasts. They had to make their way alone and wandered the countryside in search of work. But free of the need to serve a master, many ronin grew fiercely independent. In this they were unlike other samurai, whose loyalty was always to their lord.

Some ronin terrorized the peasants in rural villages. Others were hired to protect the villages or served wealthy merchants as bodyguards. Some gave lessons in *bujutsu*—the martial arts. And a few came to fame as master swordsmen. One such ronin was perhaps the most famous samurai of all: Miyamoto Musashi.

MIYAMOTO MUSASHI

Miyamoto Musashi is known today in Japan as Kensei, or "Sword Saint." He was born in 1584 and grew up under the rule of Tokugawa Ieyasu. Orphaned at age seven, Musashi was raised by an uncle, who encouraged him to study the art *of kendo*—the Way of the Sword.

A master of kendo aimed to become one with his sword—until there was no sword, no anger, no fear. A master would move without thought, treating his enemy as an honored guest, even as he cut him down.

The young Musashi was strong and aggressive. He studied sword technique, and in his first duel, at the age of 13, he killed his samurai opponent.

In Musashi's day, each daimyo kept a *dojo,* or martial arts school, where his warriors were trained. Ronin roamed the coutryside challenging the members of these schools and their teachers, or *sensei,* to duels. At 16, Musashi left home to challenge swordsmen all over Japan. By the age of 28, he had fought in more than 60 duels and had gone to war six times, fighting against Ieyasu at the Battle of Sekigahara, the largest battle ever fought between samurai.

Musashi's best known duel was with Sasaki Kojiro. Kojiro was a young samurai who had developed a new sword technique based on the movements of a swallow's tail in flight. The contest was to be held at eight in the morning on a deserted island.

The night before the duel, Musashi changed his lodgings—fueling a rumor that he was running for his life. The next morning, the officials and his opponent were assembled on the island. But Musashi did not come. An official was sent to look for him and found him asleep.

Musashi got up and without washing or dressing his hair went straight to the rowboat that was waiting to take him to the island. On the way to the duel, he tied his hair up in a towel and tied back his kimono sleeves with paper string. Then he carved a wooden sword from an extra oar and laid back to rest.

When the boat neared the shore, Musashi leaped into the water and splashed up the beach toward his enemy. Kojiro, elegantly dressed, waited very formally, then drew his long sword.

"You'll no longer have need of that," said Musashi, holding his oar down to one side. Kojiro, angered, sliced his blade downward toward Musashi. The towel binding Musashi's hair fell to the ground in two pieces, cut by Kojiro's sword. At the same moment, Musashi moved his oar upward in a single swift arc, blocking the cut, then brought his oar crashing down onto Kojiro's head. Kojiro pitched forward, his sword slicing the hem of Musashi's kimono as he fell. The young samurai was dead. Musashi stepped back. Then he bowed politely to the astonished officials and left in his boat.

After his duel with Kojiro, Musashi gave up using real swords in duels. His skill was so great he was already a legend in his own time. But at age 30, he decided that he had won all of his contests by using mere technique—not by the use of strategy. So he wandered from province to province, practicing to perfect his strategy. He is said to have been a terrible sight, because he never took a bath—he would not be caught unawares without a weapon—nor would he dress his hair or care for his clothes.

At the age of 50, he settled on the island of Kyushu, where he took up teaching, poetry, ink painting, and sculpture. For a few years, he lived as a lord's guest in a fine castle. But for the last years of his life he retired to a cave to live as a hermit. There he practiced meditation, and wrote his masterpiece, A *Book of Five Rings*, a guide to strategy that is still read today by students of kendo and business alike.

THE TALE OF THE 47 RONIN

No story better symbolizes the samurai ideals of honor, devotion and loyalty, than the *Tale of the 47 Ronin of Ako*.

In the year 1701, the shogun was planning to receive in his castle three ambassadors from

A scene from The 47 Ronin

the emperor of Japan, who would present the emperor's New Year's greeting. It was to be a formal occasion, and one that would require elaborate ceremonies.

The shogun appointed Lord Asano to lead the ceremonies. But Lord Asano, who was from the provincial town of Ako, was not familiar with the intricate customs of court. He would have to depend on advice from the shogun's Master of Court Etiquette, Kira Yoshinaka.

Lord Asano sent Kira gifts in return for his

help. Kira was not satisfied with the gifts but did not tell Lord Asano. Instead, he pretended to help but in reality would tell Lord Asano nothing, or worse, would tell him the wrong thing. Once Lord Asano arrived in court dressed in short trousers—as Kira had advised him too—only to find everyone else wearing long trousers.

Lord Asano did the best he could. But at the farewell. ceremony, he was deeply embarrassed when he stood in the wrong place. Kira would not help him. Angered, Lord Asano drew his wakizashi and slashed Kira on the forehead.

The shogun was furious—even to draw a weapon in court was a serious offense. He ordered Lord Asano to commit *seppuku,* the formal name for hara-kiri. The lord wrote his farewell poem and committed suicide. His lands were taken, and his 47 samurai became ronin.

The 47 ronin vowed they would avenge their master's death, even though they knew that the shogun would demand that they, too, would have to commit suicide if they succeeded in killing Kira. But to a samurai, life is short. Like the cherry blossoms, it blooms, then fades. More important is honor.

The Ceremony of Seppuku

Kira suspected a plot and had the men watched. So for two years, the ronin pretended to live carefree lives, drinking in taverns and visiting women. At last, Kira's spies gave up.

One snowy night, dressed in armor they had secretly had made, the 47 ronin sneaked into Kira's mansion and cut off his head. Wrapping their grisly trophy in a white cloth, they placed it on Lord Asano's grave, with a message claiming responsibility.

As they expected, the shogun ordered their

The 47 ronin take revenge.

suicide. And in 1703, the ronin carried out his order.

The people of Japan hailed the 47 ronin as heroes. They were buried next to their master, Lord Asano. Today, people still visit their tombs, and their story is told in books, plays, and films.

MUSASHI AND THE FLIES

One day, three ronin were eating supper in a country inn, when a fourth samurai sat down to eat some distance from them. His clothes were torn and dirty, and his hair was a mess. But at his belt he wore two fine swords, decorated with gold and jewels. The man looked poor, but the swords were worth a fortune. So the ronin decided they would provoke the stranger into a fight, then set upon him and rob him.

Raising their voices, they began to insult the strange samurai. "What a slob" said one. "His ancestors must have been pigs," said another. They laughed rudely.

But the stranger did not look up. He did not even seem to notice the flies buzzing around his head, as he calmly ate his rice with his chop-sticks.

The three ronin grew louder and more insult-ing. But the strange samurai just finished his rice and put his bowl aside. Then, without looking up, he struck at the air with his chop-sticks. Zip...zip...zip...zip! In four precise move-ments, he picked the flies from the air and dropped them into the bowl. There was no more buzzing.

And the inn was quiet too. For the three ron-in; recognizing a master, had run away.

The samurai, of course, was Miyamoto Musashi.

A samurai in his garden.

5

DAILY LIFE OF THE SAMURAI

A SAMURAI HOUSE AND GARDEN

Samurai houses were wooden, with high thatched roofs supported on pillars. Inside the house, light, moveable wall panels slid along grooves in the floor, so the shapes and sizes of the rooms could be changed. The heavier outer walls were made of bamboo covered with plaster. Except for the kitchen, which had an earthen floor, the wooden floors were raised off the ground to keep the house dry and airy. Floors were covered with rectangular straw mats called *tatami*. Tatami are still used today They are always the same size (about 6½ feet long by 3 feet wide.) The Japanese measure their rooms by the number of tatami it takes to cover the floors.

Samurai houses were furnished very simply, with elegant screens, low tables, and cushions. Clothing was stored in wooden chests, while bedding could be rolled and stored in cupboards.

The main room always featured a raised alcove called a *tokunoma,* in which was displayed a single object of beauty—a scroll, painting, floral arrangement, or piece of pottery—that the owner and guests could meditate upon. Samurai would use this room to receive guests and to host the tea ceremony.

The size of a samurai's house depended on his wealth and rank. A samurai's wealth was not measured in money, but in *koku*—the amount of rice his fields produced. One koku was the measure of rice it took to feed one person for one year. The peasants who farmed the fields lived in a humble village on the samurai's land. During times of war, a samurai might call upon these men to follow him into battle.

The estates of a wealthy samurai were often at risk of attack. So the complex where he lived would include a courtyard, stables for horses, and outbuildings to house his warriors. Surrounding it all he would build a high wall, and his gates would be guarded from a lookout tower by his best archers. If he suspected an attack, he would order his men to dig a moat around the walls and to dampen the roofs with mud to protect them from flaming arrows.

Whether at war or at peace, a samurai tried to find peace within himself through meditation. Often, he sought the tranquility of his garden or his private teahouse overlooking the garden. Samurai gardens were works of art, designed with flowers and trees, sunlight and shade, pools of water, or simply sand and rocks, to represent truths about the nature of life. One samurai made a garden entirely of sand. He arranged it to flow like water, to symbolize the stages of being. The sand poured from the mountainous heavens, a symbol of birth; it circled rocks and other obstacles that symbolized the challenges in the valley of life; and at last it disappeared into the earth, to a hidden end, symbolic of the mystery of death.

SAMURAI RELIGION

Japan's oldest religion is Shinto, "the way of the gods." The followers of Shinto worship spirits, or *kami,* who live in many places—rivers, forests, mountains, and caves. Kami are not really gods; rather, they are the spirits of places and objects that allow people to feel connected with all things. Shinto shrines, marked by a red gateway, or *torii,* were built in every Japanese village to honor their gods and ancestors. The spirit of the warlord Tokugawa Ieyasu was proclaimed such a kami. The most important Shinto deity is the sun goddess Amaterasu, ancestress of the emperor. Today, the Japanese reverence for their ancestors and nature, and many of their traditional customs, are rooted in Shinto.

Buddhism was brought to Japan from China in the 6th century. It soon found favor with the imperial family, who wished to temper the power of the Shinto priests. By the time of the samurai, there were several Buddhist sects. Most samurai were Zen Buddhists. Zen taught its followers to seek enlightenment and salvation within themselves, through meditation—not through the worship of a god or gods. Zen meditation took great discipline. The goal was spiritual harmony, a oneness with the flow of life and death. The ideas of Zen were especially appealing to the samurai warriors, who knew their life could end at any moment. Zen Buddhism has influenced many aspects of Japanese culture—the arts, the tea ceremony, poetry, gardening, even flower arranging.

With the arrival of Europeans in the mid-16th century, many samurai became Christians—this time, the powerful daimyo sought a way to temper the power of the Buddhist priests. But more important than any religion to the samurai was his own code, bushido—the Way of the Warrior, with its seven values: justice, courage, benevolence (generosity), politeness, honesty, honor, and loyalty.

SAMURAI EDUCATION

Samurai children were surrounded by the symbols of their warrior class from the moment of birth. During the birth of a Japanese baby, the father or a priest pulled on a bowstring so the twanging noise would frighten away evil spirits. At birth, the child was considered to be one year old.

A newborn samurai boy was given a small sword in the form of a charm to wear at his belt. At age five, he was given his first haircut, and at seven, his first wide trousers, or *hakama*. But the most important ceremony, called the *gembuku*, came at age 15, when the boy would officially become a man. He received his adult name, an adult haircut, and, best of all, his first real sword and armor.

The sons of wealthy samurai were tutored in reading, writing, and the classics of Chinese literature until the age of 10 or 12, when they were sent to study at a monastery for another four or five years.

Lessons in sword fighting, spear fighting, and archery began early. Boys were taught first by their fathers, and later perhaps by a local sensei (teacher) often a ronin. The most talented warriors might be sent to special training schools. On Boys' Festival Day (the fifth day of the fifth month) the young samurai would fight a mock battle with wooden swords. But the best training for warriors was at war—and the sons of samurai would follow their fathers into battle while still in their teens.

Samurai daughters were not formally educated. But they were sometimes allowed to listen to their brothers' lessons. As an adult, a samurai wife ran her husband's estate when he was away at war, balancing the accounts, ordering the supplies, and supervising the workers and servants.

Girls were also trained in the martial arts. Their specialty was the *yari* (straight spear) and the naginata (curved spear). Samurai women held to the same standards of honor and loyalty as samurai men.

There are many examples of samurai women who fought beside their husbands on the battlefield. The most famous was Tomoe, who fought against the Tairain the Gempei War. In one famous battle, she killed many men. The enemy leader tried to capture her and ripped the sleeve of her garment. Furious, she cut off his head and presented it to her husband.

SAMURAI FOOD AND CLOTHING

The samurai diet was quite simple. Most

Samurai boys training in the art of sword fighting.

Samurai daughters also trained in the martial arts

important were rice dishes that often included fish, vegetables, or seaweed. The most devout Buddhists did not eat meat. But in peacetime, most samurai hunted for game to eat as well. Drinks included tea and sake, a wine made from fermented rice.

Food was attractively arranged and served on low lacquer tables by the wife or a servant. It was considered very rude to breathe on another person's food, so the trays were carried high above the head.

Both men and women were very proud of their appearance. Both wore long-sleeved gowns, called *kimono*, that were belted around the waist, white cotton socks, and straw sandals or wooden clogs.

Samurai women wore several layers of kimono, each in a different color or pattern, to show their wealth. Their hair was very long and shiny. At one time, it was fashionable for women to pluck out all of their eyebrows and to paint false ones high on their forehead. It was also considered beautiful to whiten the face and to blacken the teeth.

Samurai men wore wide, skirtlike trousers called hakama over their kimono. On special occasions, they would add a jacket called a *kataginu*. The katagmu had winglike padded shoulder, and was decorated with the clan crest, or *mon*. Mature men shaved the top of their head at the front.

They bound their long hair in a ponytail, which could be folded forward onto the scalp. It was considered a disgrace ever to cut the ponytail off.

SAMURAI PASTIMES

The samurai practiced many martial arts as sports to keep them in shape for war. Matches between experts were always well attended. *Kyudo* (archery), kendo (swordsmanship), and *sumo* (wrestling) are still popular today. Swimming and hunting were also enjoyed.

Samurai attended the *noh* theater, slow-moving classical dramas based on Japanese history. But high-ranking samurai were forbidden from attending the more popular *kabuki* theater, which was noisy and colorful. Many samurai would go anyway, hiding their faces under huge, basketlike hats. Tales from the Gempei War were favorite plots. Also popular was the *bunraku,* puppet dramas acted by almost lifesize puppets. All three forms of theater are still practiced in Japan.

Samurai could learn lessons in strategy by mastering the game of *go.* Often compared to chess, go is played with black and white stones, that are placed on a square board. The object is to surround and capture the opponent's stones.

A samurai warrior was discouraged from one favorite pastime—gambling. He might survive the most ferocious battle. But if he gambled, he risked his armor, his horse, and even his sword.

A great samurai warrior was expected to have a highly developed sense of beauty. Many samurai pastimes helped him to find serenity away from the battlefield. The tea ceremony, with its strict rules for preparing and serving tea to a guest or guests, was one such pastime. It required great calm and concentration. Also popular were group cherry blossom viewings, snow viewings, and moon viewings, as well as incense contests, in which the winner identified the greatest number of smells.

More solitary occupations, all highly regarded, included painting, writing poetry, calligraphy, playing the flute, and flower arranging.

In all arts, sports, and pastimes, samurai judged the efforts of man to be most beautiful when they embodied simplicity, elegance, harmony with nature, and purity of thought.

The armor of the Samurai

6

WAYS OF THE WARRIOR

There were many ranks within a samurai army. At the top were the general and his officers. They commanded troops of cavalrymen, who rode small stocky war horses. Cavalrymen were armed with naginata and swords. Next came the archers and spearmen, who travelled on foot. Armed attendants who served the troops came last.

By the 16th century, the lower classes of warrior, or ashigaru, were trained to use light-weight firearms called *arquebuses*. An arquebus would only fire a single bullet at a time. So some groups of ashigaru trained as expert archers. Their job was to make sure the enemies' heads stayed down while the gunmen reloaded.

Samurai knew there would be no luxuries while on the road. So before going to war, they ate three lucky foods: dried shellfish, or *awabi*; *kombu*, a kind of seaweed; and chestnuts.

During wartime, samurai ate twice a day. Meals consisted of measures of rice, dried fish and vegetables, pickled plums, and seaweed. Rice was wrapped in cloth and transported raw, because once it was cooked, it would not keep well. The rice was fried or roasted in an iron war helmet that converted into a pan. Sometimes it might be dampened for cooking later. But if no water was found for cooking, the warriors had to eat dry rice.

To ready himself for battle, a samurai warlord would carefully bathe and perfume himself. Then he would dress and put on his armor. This could be an elaborate process, ending with a terrifying mask and helmet.

During the battle, the warlord would command his troops from horseback, or he would conceal himself on a hilltop behind curtains, called *maku*. In battle, the warriors could tell who was who by banners, called *sashimono*, they fastened to their armor. These were decorated with the clan crest, or mon. Officers signaled their troops by waving war fans or tasseled batons.

After a battle, high-ranking samurai often performed a tea ceremony. But another ceremony fell to the winner of the battle. It was the duty of the victorious general to review the heads of his important enemies, which had been taken as trophies. The heads were washed and their hair was combed, then they were neatly mounted on a plank for presentation.

To discourage decapitation, samurai wore iron collars and helmets with heavy neck guards. But before going into battle, the courteous samurai burned incense inside his helmet, so, in the event his head was taken, it would smell pleasant.

EQUIPMENT OF THE SAMURAI

SAMURAI ARMOR

Samurai armor was treated with the same respect and formality as a samurai sword. It was considered a grave insult, for example, to look at the inside of another's helmet.

Samurai armor was built of many scales of lacquered iron, laced together with silk or leather. The result was a suit of armor that was light—only about 25 pounds—and flexible enough to be folded and carried in a box. Just as jujitsu, a samurai form of unarmed combat, emphasized flexibility over brute force, so did Japanese armor find its strength. In contrast to the European knight in steel plate armor, who had to be hoisted onto his horse, an armored samurai could climb a castle wall, leap onto his horse, run into battle, and turn quickly to avoid a slashing sword. Armored samurai could even swim. But samurai armor did become heavy when muddy or wet, and was likely to freeze in winter and to attract lice in summer.

Putting on a suit of armor was a lengthy process. First came the undergarments: a loincloth and kimono; loose, patterned trousers; cotton or leather socks; and cotton leggings. Next came the armored shin guards, and sandals or fur boots. Leather gloves and armored sleeves were followed by a padded armpit protector. Then came the chest protector, or *cuirass*, which included skirt panels that covered the hips. A sash, or *obi*, was tied around the waist, and the katana and wakizashi (swords) thrust through. Final pieces of body armor were the shoulder guards, into which the shaft of the sashimono, or clan banner, could be fitted. If he worried that his head might be taken, a wealthy samurai might also add an iron collar.

Next the warrior would cover his head with a cotton cap to serve as padding for the heavy helmet. Then came a lacquered iron face mask, which might represent a demon, ghost, or barbarian. An old warrior might choose the mask of a young man, while a youth might want to look older and experienced. Finally came the helmet with its long neck guard. Samurai of high rank would fasten a horned crest or other ornaments to their helmets.

Over his armor, a samurai might wear a sleeveless surcoat or tentlike cape. In addition, he might carry a head bag to hold the severed head of an opponent, a provision bag, ropes used for tying or climbing, and medical supplies. All samurai were trained in wound dressing and knew how to set broken bones.

SAMURAI WEAPONS

The basic samurai weapons were the katana, a long, curved, single-edged sword, and the wak-izashi, a shorter blade used for such tasks as decapitating an enemy or performing seppuku.

But samurai warriors also made use of other kinds of blades at various periods. These included the *nodachi,* a sword that was carried slung across the back and was longer than the katana, and several sizes of dagger, called fan to and *aikuchi*

The bow and arrow were also very important. Bows came in many sizes and were made of bamboo. Arrows had reed shafts and heads of steel. Some arrowheads were perforated so they would whistle shrilly as they flew through the air. Samurai arrows could pierce even iron and steel plates.

Spears were essential in warfare. The two most common types were the naginata, or curved spear, the use of which is still studied today; and the yari, or or straight spear. Some spears were made to be thrown, like javelins. Others were hooked, for use in climbing walls or grabbing enemy armor.

Samurai also studied the use of more unusual

weapons, such as the wooden staff (bo or jo), the jitte, a dagger with sharp hooks at the hilt, and the folding iron war fan, or *gunsen*.

SAMURAI TRAINING

Samurai knew that true mastery of the martial arts involved more than physical strength and technique. Equally important were the principles of mental concentration (*haragei*), and centered, focused energy (*ki*). While a warrior practiced regular breathing to find calm and stillness within, he also learned to use his breath to explode into action with a ferocious *kiai,* or "spirit shout."

In order to help develop these skills, the warrior would practice set sequences of movements, called *kata*, over and over again, slowly at first, then with increasing speed, until they became effortless and perfect. The movements were based on strategies of attack, defense, and counterattack. They could be practiced alone with an imaginary foe or with a partner who played the role of an opponent. The techniques and movements had descriptive names. For example in kendo, or swordfighting, students, practiced the "four-sides cut," the "wheel stroke," the "thunder stroke," and the "scarf sweep."

Kata are meditative exercises as well as lessons in technique. Today, all of the martial arts use kata or similar sets of movement patterns to help train their students. Ideally, the warrior experiences a oneness of body, mind, and spirit as he moves in time and space—as if time and thought cease to exist. What remains is pure being.

Masters of the martial arts were believed to develop an almost psychic awareness of the world around them. One tale tells of a kendo master who was training his three sons. He had a guest for tea and decided to give a demonstration. He placed a vase over the door so it would fall on the head of the next person to enter the room. Then he called his youngest son, who hurried into the room. The vase fell on his head. But before it could hit the floor, the boy whipped out his sword and cut it in two.

"My youngest son has a long way to go," said the master. He put up a second vase and called his middle son. This son caught the vase in midair before it could land on his head.

"My middle son has much to learn, but he is working hard and improving," said the master.

Then he replaced the vase and called his oldest son.

The first son felt the weight of the vase as he put his hand on the door. So he slid the door open a crack, caught the vase as it fell, then opened the door the rest of the way, entered, and replaced the vase at the top of the door. The master nodded his approval. This son was doing well.

The ninja.

7

THE SAMURAI'S SECRET
WEAPON: NINJA

The samurai loved secret weapons. A favorite was a spear that looked like an innocent priest's staff. In the days of the samurai, warriors and peasants alike learned to defend themselves with everyday objects, such as fans, smoking pipes, or hairpins. They also became expert with such tools as the sickle, ax, or whirling chain. Two tools that made excellent weapons, the *tonfa* and the *nunchaku*, were originally used to husk rice and to beat grain. Study of these weapons has recently been revived in Japanese martial arts schools.

One martial art from the days of the samurai is shrouded in mystery. This is *ninjitsu,*"the art of stealth," or "the art of invisibility."

The *ninja,* practitioners of ninjitsu, were a samurai warlord's most formidable secret weapon. Ninja were expert at spying, sabotage, assassination, and escape. They used exotic weapons and trickery to accomplish their aims, methods that today seem to combine the skills of James Bond, Sherlock Holmes, and Houdini. As masters of secrecy, the ninja represented the dark side of bujutsu. They were feared but not respected and were hired to do the "dirty work"—tasks an honorable samurai, who was expected to fight openly, could not do himself,

Ninja families lived in the most wild and remote regions of Japan. Each family had its secrets, which were never revealed to outsiders. There were three ranks of ninja: leaders, who contracted with outsiders for ninja services; their assistants, or middle men; and the agents who carried out the dangerous missions. These agents were despised in Japanese society, and were tortured and executed if captured. But they were the most feared and were believed to have magical powers.

Ninja training began in earliest childhood with practice in running, jumping and climbing, swimming and diving, balancing on railings, hanging from tree limbs, and standing as still as a statue. Children were taught to dislocate their joints so they could squirm under fences or escape from knotted ropes. By the time they reached adulthood, ninja were strong, agile, and nearly immune to pain, fatigue, and cold. They could run 100 miles without resting, could walk on their hands in the dark to avoid tripping or bumping the furniture, and were expert in walking sideways, swiftly and silently, leaving no footprints. A ninja could skirt a shaded wall and never be seen.

Ninja were masters of disguise and illusion. No one knew who they were. A ninja might live as a beggar in a city, a potter in a nearby village, and a traveling actor or priest in between. A man might dress as a woman, or a woman as a man. Ninja clothing was reversible, usually dark on one side and light on the other. Ninja practiced the art of camouflage, wearing all black at night and white in the snow. A ninja in a gray cloak could roll into a ball and take the form of a rock, staying motionless for hours. He could blend in with a tree limb or a wall or could hide underwater for hours on end, breathing through a bamboo reed.

Like Sherlock Holmes, ninja were alert to clues in their surroundings. They knew, for example, that rising birds could signal an ambush. They could tell by a man's breathing if he was pretending to be asleep.

Ninja were expert in preparing medicines, including a pill that was supposed to prevent thirst for five days. They were also skilled with chemicals, drugs, poisons, and perhaps even hypnosis. Poisons could be tipped onto darts or added to an enemy food supply. Blinding acid might be blown into an enemy's face. One con- coction was an itching powder, another put enemies to sleep, and a third made them laugh uncontrollably. While the warriors were distrac- ted, the ninja would sneak over a wall or through a gate.

Ninja also made their own explosives, including small grenades and land mines. A ninja might lay a line of charges to be set off by a trip wire, to warn him of approaching enemies. To enter a house secretly, he might start a fire on the side opposite the rooms he planned to search. He might wear a horrible mask and blow fire through a tube to terrorize the enemy. Then, he might seem to disappear in a puff of smoke—a homemade smoke bomb set off to aid his escape. Poisonous smoke screens were also a ninja specialty.

Ninja often used simple trickery to gain entry to a castle or fort—dressing as a dancing girl, for example, or pretending to be sick. Once inside, they would carry out their deadly missions.

But just as often, ninja stealthily scaled the walls of a castle using special equipment. One device was a "cat claw," a band of spikes that fit across the palm of the hand, with which the ninja could even walk across a ceiling. A ninja concealed along a ceiling beam could gather much information, or even carry out an assassination.

Other climbing aids included ropes, rope ladders, and pulleys. A favorite tool was a two-bladed dagger, with one blade curved to hook on to walls or cut throats. Because they could climb anything, ninja were known as "human flies."

Ninja made use of other startling devices. They built portable boats and rafts and curious foot pontoons that they used to walk on water. They are said to have used giant kites to fly over enemy territory, sometimes dropping bombs. A winglike gliding device called the "human eagle," made of bamboo and cloth, was used to parachute behind enemy walls. And for use in castle sieges, the ninja created a kind of ferris wheel that could be loaded at the bottom and deliver ninja to the top, where they could jump over a wall one after another.

Ninja rarely used weapons that had only one purpose. A ninja sword, for example, had an extra-long, hollow scabbard that could be used as a breathing tube or blow gun, a club, or a place to conceal messages or poisons. If the sword was leaned against a wall, the hand guard, also extra-large, served as a foothold. Once atop the wall, the ninja could pull the sword up by a cord, also useful for a multitude of purposes.

Other ninja weaponry was equally ingenious. *Shuriken* were small, razor-sharp iron stars that a ninja could throw with perfect accuracy from as far as 35 feet. They came in many shapes, all deadly. Shuriken made useful tools for digging, poking, and scraping as well. Ninja carried nine different shuriken, because nine was a lucky number. There were two important techniques for throwing shuriken. First was from a stand-still, without appearing to have moved a muscle. Thus, a ninja could kill an enemy at a distance while seeming to blend in with an innocent crowd. Second was while running, so the ninja could be long gone by the time his victim fell to the ground. If he was chased, however, a ninja could reach into his pouch and throw little spikes, or *tetsu-bishi,* at the eyes and feet of his pursuers.

Many people believed the ninja were magi-cians who could change into animals or become invisible. The ninja did not discourage this idea. Instead, they thought of tricks to support peoples' superstitions. If a ninja was being hunted, for example, he might bring along a trained monkey, dressed exactly like himself. He would let his pursuers see him, and lead them into a forest. Then he would set the monkey loose and disappear up a tree. His enemies would run terrified from the forest, screaming that the ninja had transformed himself into a monkey!

Today, tales of the ninja, with their supernatural powers and impossible missions, are celebrated in Japanese films and cartoons.

Two Kendo swordsman fighting.

8

STUDYING THE MARTIAL ARTS

People who live in America, Japan, and all over the world can still study the martial arts left to us by the samurai.

There are many different martial arts systems to choose from, as well as different fighting styles within each system.

KENDO

Kendo, "the Way of the Sword," is most similar

to the training practices of an ancient samurai. *Kendoka* (kendo students) learn to fence with a lightweight bamboo sword called a *shinai*. They also wear protective armor: a helmet that looks like a baseball catcher's mask, a rounded breastplate, a hip guard, and heavy gloves.

Many Japanese students practice kendo in gym class. It is fun to play, and matches are exciting to watch. Points are scored only for strikes to four areas: the head (*men*), forearm *(kote)*, sides of the chest *(do)*, and throat *(tsuki*—only permitted for contestants over age 16). In order to score, the kendoka must step forward, shout the name of the target area to be hit (this is called the kiai), and strike, all at one time. The purpose of the kiai is to stun the opponent just for a moment. For the brief instant the opponent is frozen, the kendoka strikes.

The aim in kendo is to reach a state in which the sword, the mind, and the body are one. A true master does not think about where to strike or how to move. Rather, he must concentrate his energy and empty his mind of thought.

JUDO

Judo means "the Way of Flexibility, of Yielding." It is based on the scientific principles of resistance. A brittle branch will break in a storm, for example, but a flexible branch will bend with the wind. Likewise, a bullfighter does not try to stop a charging bull by stepping in front of it and pushing against its head. Rather, to survive, he yields—he steps aside.

In judo, the student learns to use the strength of the opponent *against* him or her. If someone strong is pushing you, for example, you can push back with all your strength—and lose. But if you *pull* the person in the same direction he is pushing, you *add* your strength to his—and will be able to throw him down.

Students of judo wear a pajamalike uniform called a *gi*, consisting of a padded jacket and drawstring trousers, tied with a belt. Belts are different colors, depending on the student's rank. Beginners wear a white belt, intermediate beginners wear a brown belt, and advanced beginners wear a black belt. It usually takes three years or more to reach this level. Many people mistakenly believe that a person with a black belt is an expert in the martial arts. In fact, there are many rankings of black belt. A low-ranking black belt is considered a serious student who has learned the basics well enough to begin to perfect his or her skill.

The floor of a judo dojo is covered with mats. Students bow before stepping onto the mats and as they leave. They also bow to the sensei (teacher) and to one another before and after their workout. Classes begin with warm-up exercise, and continue with practice in falling, called *ukemi*. Then students learn techniques of throwing and holding opponents. Advanced students practice *randori,* or "free play," in which they wrestle, as if in a competition.

Judo students also learn kata and may participate in local or even Olympic contests.

AIKIDO

Aikido, "the Way to Harmony with Ki," is a mental and spiritual discipline that teaches the power of a unified mind and body. The study of aikido can be described as "learning to free the force."

An example of how aikido works is called "the unbendable arm." Stand up and extend your arm, bent slightly at the elbow, and make a fist. Put all of your strength into it. Then ask a friend to bend your arm back toward you. You will see that your friend can do this easily, no matter how hard you resist. Next, extend your arm the same way, only relax it completely. Do not make a fist. Imagine that energy is flowing from your mind through your arm and out of your fingertips, like water in a hose. Imagine that this energy keeps on going to the ends of space. You will find that your friend can hardly move your arm—until you lose your concentration.

Many of the techniques of aikido are based on the movements of kendo and judo. But the movements are circular, with little use of kicking or punching, and are used purely for defense. There is no attack in aikido. Like judo, aikido techniques use the force of an attacker against him. But the aim is to immobilize the attacker rather than to injure or kill him.

Students of aikido wear a judo gi with a white or black belt, depending on rank. Higher-ranking students may also wear hakama, or skirtlike trousers. Classes begin with exercises, some of which are meant to help the student control his or her ki—the inner life force. Aikido students practice martial techniques by taking turns with a partner who plays the role of the attacker. They also practice with wooden swords called *bokken*.

Kung Fu

Japan was not the only country in the East to develop systems of martial arts. In fact, many of the techniques used by the samurai were inspired by a Chinese system of self-defense called *kung fu*. Kung fu was the specialty of the warrior monks of the Shaolin monastery, home of the founder of Zen Buddhism. Movements in the many styles of kung fu are based on the ways of animals: the sturdy posture of the horse, the one-legged stance of the white crane, the defenses of a praying mantis, the antic movements of a monkey.

Teachers of kung fu are called *sifus*. Students train with and without weapons, learning to strike, block, and kick. Kung fu katas are called "sets." Students of kung fu also study the principles of *ch'i*—the breath or inner life force called ki in Japanese.

Karate and Tae Kwon Do

Karate, or "empty hands fighting," was developed on the island of Okinawa, off the coast of China. The islanders had no swords or spears. So they learned to defend themselves with their hands and feet instead. Karate is the martial art we think of when we picture someone karate chopping a stack of boards. But this is merely a demonstration. Karate students learn to punch and kick, concentrating their energy with a kiai.

Students wear a lightweight gi, and practice kata that look like dance routines. They also learn to spar.

The Korean style of karate is called *tae kwon do*. Today, both karate and tae kwon do are studied worldwide.

The last Tokugawa Shogun

9

THE SAMURAI LEGACY

The Tokugawa shoguns ruled Japan for more than 250 years. The country was at peace, completely cut off from the rest of the world. But the military threat of the West, coupled with the superiority of Western technology in the mid-19th century, were more than the samurai could resist. In 1853, Commodore Matthew Perry, an American naval officer, arrived in Japan and forced its opening to Western trade. Soon afterward, the power of the last Tokugawa shogun collapsed, and in 1868, the rule of Japan was restored to the Emperor Meiji. In 1876, the government of Japan banned the wearing of swords by anyone who was not a member of the imperial armed forces. The seat of government was moved to Tokyo, and Japan's modern constitution was adopted. The days of the samurai were over.

But the spirit of the samurai lives on in Japan to this day. The values of bushido—honor, loyalty, and self-sacrifice—were nowhere more evident than among the military during World War II. Western soldiers were stunned by the seemingly pointless bravery of the Japanese soldiers. Officers armed only with swords charged enemy machine gunners and were mowed down. Kamikaze pilots, named for the divine winds that had saved their country against foreign invaders so long ago, flew suicide missions, crashing their planes onto enemy ships. Equally disturbing to Westerners was the cruel treatment prisoners-of-war received from their Japanese captors, who believed that the captured soldiers had lost their honor.

Loyalty to one's family and superiors is deeply ingrained in Japanese culture. Modern Japanese show the same loyalty to their employers that their samurai ancestors once showed their lords.

Suicide is still considered an acceptable response to disgrace.

Tales of samurai heroes are very much alive in modern Japan, in movies, plays, ghost stories, novels, comic books, cartoons, and video games. The faces of samurai appear on toys and kites, on menus and posters.

Some of the most famous samurai movies are also popular in America. The best known of these films, *The Seven Samurai,* was even made into a Western version, called *The Magnificent Seven.*

The ideas of Zen and the discipline of the martial arts have captured the American imagination as well. One example is the story of *Star Wars*, in which a young warrior, Luke Skywalker, must seek a master, who he finds in a mysterious forest. The gnomelike master, Yoda, is similar to the tengu goblins who taught the hero Yoshitsune. Yoda teaches young Skywalker to master a swordlike weapon, by harnessing The Force"—a mental and spiritual energy that is similar to the Japanese ki.

"Concentrate!" Yoda urges his young student.

After much study, hard work, and dedication, Luke becomes an excellent warrior and is able to defeat his enemies.

Today, the fine arts of the samurai are still practiced in Japan, including calligraphy, flower arrangement, and the tea ceremony. Although these arts have gained some popularity in the West, it is the martial arts of Japan—judo, kendo, and aikido—that are most widely studied. The legacy of the samurai lives on.

Three kung fu positions.

A Painting of a medieval Japanese battle

The Fourth Battle of Kawanakajima

October 1561

In 1490 Japan entered a crucial period of its history known as the *sengoku-jidai*, or the "Age of the Country at War." For the next century and a half scarcely a year would pass without a battle or a campaign raging somewhere in the country. The daimyo, or "great names" (erroneously referred to as warlords), who controlled the numerous provinces of Japan, began to vie with one another to increase their domains and the power of their family clans. For a few, those who had the military power and the political strength to challenge, was a chance to become shogun, the military ruler of Japan.

By the middle of the 16th century, warfare in Japan significantly changed, influenced to a great extent by the ever increasing struggle between the competing daimyo. The samurai armies of the daimyo began to increase in size, augmented by the addition of the "ashigaru", (or "light-feet") trained, well disciplined peasant foot soldiers. Castles began to take on a greater military prominence as a means of controlling an area and as a secure base for military supplies and troops. Lastly, an invention from Europe, the firearm, begins to appear in samurai armies from 1540 onwards.

The power of the daimyo, and thus the power of his clan, stemmed from the territories or provinces they controlled. Their economic wealth was measured by the agricultural production of their lands, and was assessed in "koku." A koku was the amount of rice it took to feed one man for one year. Koku provided the system of measuring the yearly yield of the rice fields and also determined the number of soldiers the daimyo could raise, arm and feed to defend his lands. From these lands also came the men who would form the daimyo's army. The samurai, essentially hereditary vassals and retainers of the lord and his clan, were expected to raise and equip a predetermined number of troops from the clan domains they controlled. These would include other samurai of lesser rank as well as the ashigaru. When the daimyo's army conquered another province or territory, his loyal samurai could expect an increase in their domains, which would in turn increase their personal wealth and the number of men they would now be expected to raise from that domain. The conquest of another territory also meant that a daimyo could increase his wealth and military strength by either making the conquered lord a vassal, thus securing his army and his wealth, or by striking an alliance with the conquered lord for his support in future military operations. Under such a system it is understandable why the daimyo became so fiercely engaged in territorial expansion. One of the more interesting examples of such territorial warfare was between the daimyo's of the Echigo and Kai provinces.

In 1553 an intense power struggle began between the Takeda clan of Kai Province, under the leadership of Takeda Shingen, and the Murakami and Nagao clans of Echigo Province, under Uesugi Kenshin. This conflict resulted in a long-standing military rivalry between these two daimyo which lasted until 1564. In 1547 Shingen led the Takeda clan on an invasion of Shinano Province, a rich territory which lay between the western border of Kai and the southern border of Echigo Province. In lieu of being destroyed by the powerful Takeda army, some of the Shinano daimyo, such as the Sanada, submitted to the invader and became Shingen's vassals. Many of the other Shinano daimyo's were determined to resist the invaders, the most noted of these being Murakami Yoshikiyo. In 1548 Shingen defeated Murakami in a bloody battle at Ueda-hara. Realizing that he could not withstand Shingen's power alone, Murakami appealed for aid from his northern neighbor, Uesugi Kenshin, Lord of Echigo Province. Kenshin agreed to give his assistance to Murakami, and with this alliance the two powerful clans of Takeda and Uesugi were brought into direct conflict.

In assembling the army to aid Murakami, Kenshin sent out the "kashindan," or "call to arms." This, it seems, was usually in the form of a detailed letter, sent to all the loyal retainers of the clan. Among the reasons given for calling out the army, there would also be included a listing of their record of obligations, such as the number of troops by type they were to provide, the arms and supplies, and where they were to concentrate their forces. A good example of a surviving kashindan, written by Uesugi Kenshin to Irobe Katsunaga, his "gun-bugyo," or "chief of staff," is given below, and aptly describes the situation brought on by Shingen's invasion of Shinano province.

"Concerning the disturbances among the various families of Shinano and the Takeda of Kai in the year before last, it is the honorable opinion of Imagawa Yoshimoto of Sumpu that things must have calmed down. However, since this time, Takeda Harunobu's (Takeda Shingen's previous name) example of government has been corrupt and bad. However, through the will of the gods and from the kind offices of Yoshimoto, I, Kagetora (Kenshin's previous name) have very patiently avoided any interference. Now, Harunobu has recently set out for war and it is a fact that he has torn to pieces the retainers of the Ochiai family of Shinano and Katsurayama castle has fallen. Accordingly, he has moved into the so-called Shimazu and Ogura territories for the time being.... My army will be turned in this direction and I, Kagetora will

set out for war and meet him half way. In spite of snowstorms or any sort of difficulty we will set out for war by day or night. I have waited fervently. If our family's allies in Shinano can be destroyed then even the passes of Echigo will not be safe. Now that things have come to such a pass, assemble your pre-eminent army and be diligent in loyalty, there is honorable work to be done at this time.
With respects,

Kenshin,
1557, 2nd month, 16th day"

In the far northern reaches of Shinano Province, located deep in the heart of the mountain range known as the Japan Alps, lay the wide, flat, triangular shaped plain of Kawanakajima. Known as "the island between the rivers," because it was bordered on the north by the Saigawa River and on the southwest by the Chikumagawa River which join at the northeast corner of the plain, Kawanakajima became the no man's land in the duel between Shingen and Kenshin. During the course of their struggle this plain would witness no less than seven encounters between these rivals, of which only five were considered "battles." The first three of these battles were only preliminary skirmishes compared to the fourth, which is considered "the" battle of Kawanakajima, and remains one of the largest and bloodiest conflicts in Japanese history.

In September 1553, Shingen advanced far to the north of Shinano Province, reaching the Kawanakajima plain. Here, near a Hachiman shrine, he met Kenshin's army, but refused battle and withdrew. The two armies came into contact a few miles farther north, but again disengaged from each other. This was the First Battle of Kawanakajima, also known as "The Battle of Fuse." In October, as Shingen was withdrawing from the area, Kenshin attacked near the site of the Hachiman shrine and defeated the Takeda army.

The Second Battle of Kawanakajima, also known as "The Battle of the Saigawa," took place in 1555. Shingen advanced across the Kawanakajima plain to the Saigawa River and made his camp on the Otsuka hill, just south of the river. Kenshin's army moved from their hill positions down to the river and camped on the opposite bank. For four months the two armies sat facing one another, waiting for the other to make the first move. Eventually, faced with political unrest among their allies, both armies withdrew.

The Third Battle of Kawanakajima took place in 1557. Shingen again advanced onto the plain and captured Katsurayama, a mountain fortress deep in Uesugi territory. He then attacked Iiyama Castle, which lay along a major road into Echigo and northeast of the Zenko-ji, a hill-top position which a dominant view of the entire plain. Kenshin, whose army was based in Zenko-ji Castle and responded by launching a sortie to relieve Iiyama castle. Shingen promptly withdrew, once again avoiding a major battle with his enemy.

In September 1561, the two armies engaged in the Fourth Battle of Kawanakajima. Kenshin, weary of the sparring with Shingen, resolved to destroy his arch-rival in one last decisive battle and marched his army of 18,000 towards the north-western periphery of Takeda territory. His objective was Kaizu Castle which controlled Takeda communications north onto the plain of

Kawanakajima and south of the plain through the vital mountain passes. Crossing the Saigawa and Chikumagawa Rivers which enclose Kawanakajima, Kenshin took up a fortified position on Saijoyama Mountain overlooking Kaizu Castle. The 150 samurai and their followers who garrisoned Kaizu, although thoroughly surprised by this move, managed, through a system of well organized signal fires, to alert Shingen of the danger. Shingen reacted quickly and moved towards Kaizu with 16,000 men.

Upon reaching Kawanakajima, Shingen camped on the west bank of the Chikumagawa River near the Amenomiya Ford. Kenshin had hoped to be in a position to fall on his enemy upon the latter's arrival, but with the river between them a stalemate now ensued. An element of surprise was needed to throw one side off balance if the other were to succeed. Shingen moved first, quickly crossing the Chikumagawa beneath Kenshin's positions and moving his entire force, increased by reinforcements to 20,000, into Kaizu Castle.

Shingen's force would not remain here long, however, as his gun-bugyo, Yamamoto Kansuke, had devised an interesting plan known as Operation "Woodpecker." A "woodpecker" force of 8,000 men would climb Saijoyama under cover of night and "tap" Kenshin's rear, driving the enemy "bugs" out of their positions, down the mountain and across the Chikumagawa onto the Hachimanabara, or "War God Plain," below. Here, Shingen's main body, having also crossed the Chikumagawa by night, would be waiting for them. The formation Shingen chose for his main body was the *kakuyoku*, or "crane's wing," which was considered to be the best formation for surrounding an enemy. Driven by the attack against his rear into the arms of the "crane's wing" Kenshin would be caught between two forces, surrounded and destroyed.

The "crane's wing" formation was deployed as follows:

> "A screen of arquebusiers and archers protect the vanguard while the main body of samurai, forming a second and third division, are spread out behind them like the swept-back wings of a crane. The general's headquarters occupy the centre, protected on both sides by *hatamoto* (meaning "under the standard"), the particular chosen

samurai. A squadron of reserve troops stand on each side, slightly to the rear of the hatamoto. There is a rearguard, with more archers and arquebusiers."

Shingen set up his headquarters in the center of the Hachiman Plain, somewhere in the rear of the samurai wings. This command post consisted of a *maku*, or cloth curtains, bearing the Takeda *mon*, or clan badge, making it easily identifiable to all. From this position he waited for his plan to be put into motion.

As dawn broke the next day Shingen's troops, peering through the dispersing mist, were met by the sight of Kenshin's army not fleeing across their front, as planned, but charging head on towards them. Kenshin, having received reports on Shingen's movements, had guessed what his rival's plan might be and had accordingly planned a counter-maneuver. Using the cover of night as had his enemy, Kenshin had moved his army in total secrecy across the Amenomiya ford, leaving a 3,000 man rearguard to protect the ford, and deployed somewhat west of Shingen's position.

Adopting a formation known as *kuruma gakari*, or "winding wheel," Kenshin crashed violently into Shingen's "crane." The "winding wheel" was an offensive maneuver which allowed units which had become exhausted or depleted through combat to be replaced with a fresh unit, thus enabling the attacker to maintain the force and momentum of the attack. A very carefully organized and complex maneuver, its use indicates that Kenshin's troops must have practiced it to the point of perfection. Kenshin's vanguard was commanded by his younger brother, Takeda Nobushige, and as Kenshin's "winding wheel" fully engaged the Takeda front ranks, Nobushige was killed in the desperate close combat.

Kenshin's leading units were mounted samurai, and as the "wheel" wound on, the pressure on Shingen's force began to tell as unit after unit was driven back from its positions. Shingen's "crane" was an offensive formation and not designed for the defense, but the troops executing it were well disciplined and the formation was managing to hold its own. Realizing that his well laid plans had failed, Yamamoto Kansuke accepted responsibility for the disaster in true samurai fashion. Charging alone with a spear into the midst of the enemy he fought valiantly until overcome by some eighty wounds, whereupon he retired to a grassy knoll and committed hara-kiri.

The momentum of the "wheel" had by now brought it within reach of the Takeda headquarters where Shingen had been fervently trying to control his hard pressed army. The Uesugi samurai clashed head on with Shingen's hatamoto and personal bodyguard, wounding his son Takeda Yoshinobu. A single mounted samurai then crashed through the maku curtains and Shingen suddenly found himself personally attacked by none other than Kenshin himself. Unable to draw his sword in time, Shingen, rising from his camp stool, was forced to parry Kenshin's mounted sword strokes with his heavy wooden war fan. Shingen took three cuts on his body armor and a further seven on his war fan until one of his bodyguard charged forward and attacked Kenshin with a spear. The spear thrust glanced off Kenshin's armor and struck his horse's flank, causing the animal to rear. Several other samurai of Shingen's guard then arrived and together they managed to drive Kenshin off. The site of this famous skirmish is now called *mitachi nana tachi no ato* ("three sword seven sword place"), and next to it is a fine modern statue depicting the fight between the two generals."

Shingen's "crane" was slowly being driven back on the Chikumagawa River and his best samurai were falling all around, but despite the fierceness of the constantly rotating attacks the formation had not yet broken. Just as Kenshin seemed assured of victory he was suddenly surprised by a desperate attack against his rear. The Takeda "woodpecker" force, having found the enemy positions on Saijoyama deserted and hearing the noise of battle below, had moved down to the Amenomiya Ford. Here they engaged Kenshin's rearguard in the fiercest fighting of the day, driving them back and crossing the river to assault Kenshin's rear. Kenshin's force was thus caught between the pincers of the Takeda attack, just as the late Yamamoto Kansuke had planned. Shingen managed to regain control of his army and by midday what had seemed an inglorious defeat had been turned into a great victory. Some of Shingen's troops even managed to reclaim the head of Nobushige, Shingen's brother, as well as the heads of several other leading Takeda samurai from the Uesugi warriors who had taken them as trophy's. Shingen's army, exhausted from the battle, did not attempt to pursue Kenshin's retreat. The following day, under a truce, some of Kenshin's generals burned what was left of their encampment on Saijoyama while the rest of the army moved back across the Saigawa and headed for home.

Kawanakajima had been a costly battle for both sides. Kenshin had lost 72%, or roughly 12,960 men, while Shingen, although taking 3,117 enemy heads as trophies, had lost 62%, or 12,400 men. In one of the largest battles ever fought in Japanese history, the "crane's wing" formation, when executed by well disciplined troops, had proven itself capable of stopping, at least temporarily, that of the "winding wheel."

In September 1564 the two rivals met again for the fifth and final battle at Kawanakajima. Facing each other across the Saigawa River the respective armies sat in their positions for sixty days, engaging in only minor skirmishing, before finally withdrawing.

The battles at Kawanakajima stand as a fascinating example of both the style of clan warfare which typified the sengoku-jidai period as

well as the type of highly ornate and complicated tactics employed by the armies. The ability
to perform complex maneuvers by night and
then assemble into such large and intricately
designed tactical formations speaks volumes for
the high degree of training, discipline, and
weapons specialization clearly evidenced by the
armies of the daimyo. (A good and fairly historic
example of the battles of Kawanakajima, the
rivalry between Shingen and Kenshin, and the
tactics employed by the armies can be seen in
the Japanese film production *Heaven and Earth*.)

Takeda Shingen

Born Harunobu Takeda in 1521, he was the
eldest son of Takeda Nobutora, daimyo, or bar-
on, of Kai province. The Takeda were an ancient
family descended from Minamoto Yoshimitsu,
whose son, Yoshikiyo, was the first to take the
surname Takeda. During the Gempei Civil War,
Yoshikiyo supported the leader of the Minamoto
clan, Minamoto Yoritomo, against the Taira clan.
Minamoto Yoritomo's subsequent victory resulted in his becoming the first Shogun, or military
ruler, of Japan. As a consequence of their sup-

port, the Takeda family became very powerful in their region of Japan.

Takeda Nobutora, a very capable samurai leader, established himself as a feudal lord and began a policy of territorial expansion. In 1540 he was deposed by his son, Harunobu, in an effort to prevent the latter's own displacement by a younger brother. Harunobu had his baptism of fire at the age of 15, when he rescued his father and won the day in an engagement at Uminokuchi fortress in 1536. This action set the stage of Harunobu's future military prowess.

In 1547, Harunobu, continuing his father's program of expansion, invaded Shinano province. Significant resistance to Takeda incursions was offered by Murakami Yoshikiyo, who had once fought against Harunobu's father. Harunobu defeated Murakami at Ueda-hara in 1548, and the latter, realizing that he could not withstand the advances of the son as he had the father, enlisted the aid of Uesugi Kenshin, the young and powerful lord of Echigo province. For the next 17 years Harunobu and Kenshin, both of relatively equal military skill, would be in a state of almost constant war with one another. In 1551 Harunobu became a Buddhist monk and took the name of "Shingen," by which he was generally known thereafter.

In 1553 Shingen fought the first of five battles against Uesugi Kenshin at Kawanakajima. The first three of these battles were little more than skirmishes in which the two opponents matched the developing skills of themselves and their armies against one another. The Fourth Battle of Kawanakajima in October 1561 was a large scale engagement in which Shingen, although wounded and initially in a bad position, eventually emerged as the victor after a fierce and bloody struggle. Following the fifth and final battle of Kawanakajima in 1564, Kenshin had ceased to be a serious threat to Shingen's power.

Their long standing rivalry, however, had almost become legend, adding to the fame of both their names. Due to their constant interaction through warfare, both men had developed a great deal of respect for one another. "The respect in which Kenshin and Shingen held each other is best illustrated by the famous 'salt incident.' As Shingen's provinces lay in the mountains he was consequently dependent upon the good offices of the Hojo (clan) for the supply of salt. During one of the Kawanakajima campaigns the current Hojo cut off Shingen's salt supply. Kenshin, hearing of Shingen's dilemma, commented that Hojo had performed a very mean act, and sent Shingen some salt from his own province, which bordered on the Sea of Japan. He added, 'I do not fight with salt, but with the sword.'"

In 1568 Shingen attacked and drove the weaker Imagawa clan from Suruga province, but was unable to maintain his hold against the attacks of the Hojo clan from the east. Becoming ever more concerned with the growing power and military accomplishments of Oda Nobunaga, leader of Owari province, Shingen realized that he would soon have to confront this new rival.

In 1571 Nobunaga attacked and destroyed the Buddhist monastery at Mount Hiei, thus giving Shingen, a Buddhist monk, just the excuse he needed. In October 1572 Shingen attacked Nobunaga's ally, Tokugawa Ieyasu at Mikata-ga-hara. Shingen soundly defeated Ieyasu's numerically inferior force, but failed to follow up his victory. In early 1573 Shingen, now resolved to destroy Ieyasu, attacked the latter in his castle at Noda. According to legend, the defenders of Noda Castle, knowing that their end was near, decided to dispose of their stocks of sake (rice wine) by drinking them. The noises of their celebration were noted by the besiegers, as was the excellent flute playing of one of the castle's garrison. Shingen, approaching the ramparts to listen to the music, was shot in the head and killed by a vigilant castle guard. The Takeda clan kept the news of Shingen's death secret for as long as they could (reputedly for more than a year) in an effort to deceive Nobunaga and his allies. Eventually, the news leaked out and Shingen's son, Katsuyori, took his father's place in the ongoing struggle with Nobunaga. But Katsuyori was not the military commander his father was. At Nagashino in June 1575, Katsuyori impetuously launched the cream of the Takeda army against the prepared positions of their enemy. They were wiped out by Nobunaga's massed arquebusiers, thus crushing Takeda power forever.

Shingen stands as one of the greatest as well as one of the most terrible personalities during the "Age of the Country at War" (Sengoku-jidai) period of Japanese history. A skillful and competent ruler, Shingen was renown for both his military prowess and his personal magnetism.

Possessing great energy and intelligence he was both shrewd and ruthless, cruel and magnanimous. Famous for his ability to rally people to his banners, he increased the power and standing of the Takeda clan to its greatest heights, only to die prematurely. Although he had the talents necessary to unify Japan, his long rivalry with Uesugi Kenshin diverted much of his energy and efforts from this cause. Without the wisdom and skill of his leadership the power of the Takeda clan was eventually destroyed under his son.

Oda Nobunaga

The Battle of Nagashino

June 29, 1575

Throughout the course of military history, the introduction of new or improved technology on the battlefield has resulted not only in a necessary change in tactics, but often in a dramatic change in the nature and conduct of warfare itself. The Battle of Nagashino serves as a dramatic and fascinating example of the affects of technology on both warfare and on a society steeped in a warrior-based culture.

The Battle of Nagashino, which took place on June 29 1575, was fought toward the end of that period of Japanese history known as Sengoku-jidai, or the "Age of the Country at War," which lasted from 1477 to 1576. It is disturbingly ironic, especially considering the resulting consequences, that this battle, purely from a strategic perspective, was really quite unnecessary.

The battle was the end result of an unsuccessful siege of Nagashino Castle, a frontier castle which, with others, formed a defensive net against invasion through the Takeda Mountains. The castle was defended by 500 Tokugawa retainers, allies of Oda Nobunaga, one of the strongest and most able daimyos of this period. The besieging force was some 15,000 strong and led by Takeda Katsuyori, the brave but head-strong son of Takeda Shingen, the recently deceased head of the Takeda clan and long time enemy of Nobunaga. Katsuyori, in a continu-ation of his father's forward policy against the Takeda clan's enemies, planned to take Nagashino Castle and invade further into Tok-ugawa territory, thus gaining more provinces and strengthening his military position. Origin-ally, the castle was supposed to fall by betrayal from within, but when the plan was discovered Katsuyori found himself on facing a major siege operation. Although the castle's defenders were inferior in numbers, the castle itself was strongly built and well situated for prolonged defense. Their one weak point was food. A messenger managed to reach Nobunaga to request help or witness the castle's fall.

Nobunaga, fearing that failure to aid his new allies might drive them back into the arms of the Takeda, immediately began marching to the castle's aid with an army of 38,000 men, 10,000 of whom were his teppo-shu, or arquebus corps. By the time Katsuyori reached Nagashino Castle on June 16, he had already conducted a successful campaign and, on hearing of Nobunaga's approach, could have simply retired and consolidated his new conquests. Although many explanations have been set forth attempting to explain Katsuyori's decision to remain—that the father had once taken the castle with ease and the son desired to outdo him, or that Katsuyori wished to display his ability by also defeating his father's old enemy—there is no doubt that the capture of Nagashino had become an obsession for him. Regardless of the reasons, Katsuyori moved to meet Nobunaga on the hilly Shitarabara Plain below Nagashino Castle.

Nobunaga, having previously experienced to his regret the devastating effect of a Takeda cavalry charge, devised his battle plan with the express purpose of negating such a thrust. First, he positioned his army so that the Takeda would have to cross two streams to reach his front. He then erected loose palisades along his front behind which he positioned 3,000 handpicked men from his arquebus corps arranged in three

1,000-man lines. Further, Nobunaga placed a small detachment outside the palisades on his right to draw the Takeda toward him. Nobunaga's plan was to break the charge of the Takeda cavalry and then, once they were stopped by the fire from the arquebusiers, he would launch his samurai through the gaps in the palisades and descend on the remnants of the enemy and destroy them. On the evening of June 28, Sakai Tadatsuga led 3,000 men in a disruption raid on the Takeda camp in which Katsuyori's uncle, Takeda Nobuzane, one of the army's section commanders, was killed.

At 5 A.M. on June 29, the Takeda took the bait and launched a series of cavalry charges against Nobunaga's lines. A feigned retreat by Sakuma Morimasa's men on Nobunaga's left flank further enticed the Takeda to attack. The arquebusiers began a sustained volley fire by ranks which shattered the Takeda charge. Nobunaga's samurai then counterattacked from behind the palisades, falling on the Takeda and driving them back. Again the Takeda charged, and again the arquebusiers stopped them and the Oda samurai counterattacked and drove them back. By about midday even the headstrong Katsuyori realized that the battle was irrevocably lost and he ordered a retreat. Scattered across Shitarabara Plain lay over 10,000 dead, the flower of the Takeda cavalry. Furthermore, seven of the Takeda's twenty-four generals were killed, seriously damaging the magnificent command staff established by Takeda Shingen. Nobunaga's losses were roughly 6,000 men.

Nagashino sounded the death knell of the once great Takeda clan. Although they were able to forestall the inevitable for another seven years, Takeda power was broken and no longer a match for the combined forces of the Oda and Tokugawa clans. In 1582 Katsuyori, his army reduced to only 300 men, fought his last battle at Torii-bata Pass, preferring suicide to capture by his family's arch enemy.

In *Battles of the Samurai*, author Stephen Turnbull states, "...If Nagashino had been Oda Nobunaga's only victory his reputation would have been secured. Instead it is the culmination of a brilliant career, and a milestone in Japanese history." Nobunaga's innovative use of field fortifications and massed, volley fire changed forever the course of warfare in feudal Japan. Most significant, was the fact that Nobunaga's

arquebus corps was composed entirely of ashigaru, or peasant soldiers, the samurai refusing
to lower themselves by using such a weapon.
This caused a sensation amongst the samurai
class because now any peasant with a modicum
of firearm training could effectively kill a
samurai long before the latter could get close
enough to retaliate, thereby neutralizing a lifetime dedicated to military training. While
Nobunaga gained both military fame and cen-
sure for the quality of training he gave his ashigaru, he also unknowingly set in motion events
which would lead to the general disarmament
of the country in 1587, and finally culminate
in Japan "giving up the gun" about 1637. The
Japanese would experience another major disruption of their society due to technological
influence from the west on August 6 1945, at
Hiroshima. In this case, the result was more than
"giving up the gun," it was the wholesale
renouncement of war itself.

Oda Nobunaga

By the time of his death in 1582, he controlled
thirty of Japan's sixty-eight provinces, was the

commander of the greatest samurai army in his country's history, and had earned the distinction of being the first of the three great unifiers of Japan. Imbued with a driving ambition he was ruthless and cruel, often to both to friends and foes alike. He displayed a genuine talent for administration and developed a reputation which caused him to be both feared and admired. Possessing a keen military mind his daring tactical innovations would ultimately alter the course of Japanese warfare.

His name was Oda Nobunaga and he was born in 1534 in the province of Owari, near Nagoya, to a daimyo family. At the age of 23 Nobunaga demonstrated both his military ability and his burning desire to become a great daimyo by relentlessly driving his older and more popular brother from their home province. Thus he began a career which would last for the next quarter century.

One of Nobunaga's first and greatest tactical triumphs was at Okehazama on June 22, 1560. When his province was invaded by Yoshimoto Imagawa's huge 25,000 man army, Nobunaga, instead of retreating or taking refuge in one of his fortresses, opted instead to attack. With only around 3,000 men at his disposal, Nobunaga was forced to rely on deception and surprise. Operating in hilly, forested terrain, Nobunaga was able to create the illusion of a large army by covering the summit, just below the reverse brow, of a carefully chosen hill with hundreds of war banners. Operating on familiar terrain, he was then able to circumvent the enemy position and approach from the north. A fortuitous thunderstorm screening his army's final approach, Nobunaga launched a violent attack from the enemy's rear. Although outnumbered nearly ten-to-one, Nobunaga caught the enemy completely by surprise, surrounded and killed Yoshimoto in his own headquarters, and completely routed the Imagawa army. With their commander dead, the Imagawa withdrew to their own lands, leaving Nobunaga's province safe.

One of the former Imagawa generals, impressed with Nobunaga's victory, entered into an alliance with him. This was Tokugawa Ieyasu, who would become one of Nobunaga's best allies and whose family would hold the title of shogun in Japan for 265 years. Realizing the necessity of strong alliances, Nobunaga, himself married to the daughter of the Mino daimyo, a neighboring province, married his sister and daughter to other powerful daimyo, thus securing more allies and further consolidating his position.

Nobunaga then began a series of campaigns of conquest with the design of unifying Japan under one banner. In 1567 he destroyed the Saito clan and the following year he conquered the Ise and Omi provinces. On November 9, 1568, he entered Kyoto and reestablished Yoshiaki Ashikaga to his position as shogun. Defeated while attempting to conquer Echizen Province in 1570, he nevertheless turned north and defeated a coalition of his enemies at Anegawa on July 22 of that year. Enraged by the fierce resistance of the Buddhists, Nobunaga destroyed their monastery on Mount Hiei, forever crushing their political power in Japan. Discovering that Yoshiaki was plotting with his enemies against him, Nobunaga deposed the Shogun, thus ending the dynasty of the Ashik-aga Shoguns. Throughout 1573-74, Nobunaga attempted, with only partial success, in checking the Ikko-Ikki sectarians. On June 29, 1575, Nobunaga won his greatest victory at Nagashino against the Takeda clan. His imaginative and revolutionary use of peasant arquebusiers whose utilization of volley fire enabled them to defeat mounted samurai caused both a tactical and social sensation amongst the daimyo of Japan.

In 1579 Nobunaga again campaigned against the Ikko-Ikki, this time securing their surrender in April 1580. In 1582 he finished the job he had begun at Nagashino by destroying the Takeda clan and causing the suicide of their daimyo, Katsuyori, at Temmoku San. Answering a call for assistance from one of his generals, Toyotomi Hideyoshi, Nobunaga sent all available reinforcements. This move, however, left him dangerously vulnerable. On April 22, 1582, Nobunaga was ambushed by Akechi Mitsuhide, one of his own generals, while in the Honno-ji temple in Kyoto. His bodyguard surprised and slaughtered, Nobunaga fought on alone. Realizing the situation was hopeless and with the temple burning around him, Nobunaga committed suicide rather than be taken captive. Upon hearing the news of Nobunaga's death, the townspeople looted and then burned to the ground his magnificent castle at Azuchi.

Although unable to attain the title of shogun himself, due to his humble birth, Nobunaga's conquests instead helped to establish the Tokugawa clan as hereditary military rulers of Japan for over two centuries, and began the process of Japanese unification. His innovative use of massed arquebusiers at Nagashino also had far reaching consequences. Worried not only over the future affects of such weapons on their long established traditions of warfare, but also over the possibility of class rebellion, the daimyos attempted to control the use and manufacture of firearms. In 1587 Lord Hideyoshi, then regent of Japan, began a policy of disarmament which would eventually lead to the abandonment of firearms altogether. For over two centuries after his death, Japan continued to feel the impact of Oda Nobunaga's great achievements.

Toyotomi Hideyoshi was responsible for the second stage of consolidation in Japan

A Return to Traditional Ways

Medieval Japan's Renouncement of Firearm Technology

Since the appearance of the first weapon and its practical application as a tool for war, mankind in general has striven to produce better, more effective weapons for its armies. This was particularly the case after the discovery of gunpowder and the subsequent development of firearms. Firearm technology continues to proceed apace, with newer models possessing an even greater rate of fire than their predecessors and made from such diverse elements as plastics and ceramics.

With only one particular exception, firearm development has always moved forward with the singular purpose of making a better weapon for soldiers than they one they had before. The one unique exception to this steadfast rule was Japan in the 16th and 17th centuries. Japan, having initially discovered firearms from visiting Europeans, quickly became fascinated with the capabilities of such a weapon. By employing their superb craftsman and superior metal working abilities the Japanese proceeded to develop firearm technology to a degree far surpassing that employed in Europe. After having utilized firearms for nearly a century, a series of consequential events caused the Japanese to reevaluate their attitude toward the weapon. They then began a nationwide disarmament policy, eventually resulting in the complete abandonment of firearms throughout the country. The Japanese had essentially defied the "status quo" of firearm technology and gone in the opposite direction by "giving up the gun."

The Japanese were first introduced to firearms, in the form of the matchlock arquebus, by three Portuguese adventurers in 1543. The timing was apropos, as the arquebus arrived in the middle of a century long power struggle in Japan and the rival warlords were extremely interested in any new weapon which might give them a decisive edge. Japanese swordsmiths were subsequently put to work reproducing the arquebus.

Within a decade of its appearance the arquebus was being produced in the thousands by gunsmiths who had sprung up throughout the country. Furthermore, these were high quality weapons, not just simple imitations. Since Japan had been a leading manufacturer of weapons for over two hundred years—in 1483, a definite landmark year, she exported some 67,000 swords to China alone—it was a relatively easy task to include firearms to an already existing array of fine quality weapons. Not only did the Japanese demonstrate their ability to copy the arquebus, but by applying their superior metal working and craftsmanship skills to the task, they significantly improved the basic design. They developed a helical main spring and an adjustable trigger pull, increased the caliber for greater effectiveness against armor, developed a serial firing technique to increase the flow of ammunition, designed special waterproof lacquer cases for gun and ammunition, as well as a waterproof box-like cover for the matchlock to enable the weapon to be fired in the rain! But most significant was the skill displayed in the making of the barrels. Many of these arquebuses, having been retired after generations of use in the 16th and 17th centuries, were brought out and converted to percussion rifles in the late 1850's, and then converted yet again to bolt-action rifles for use in the war against Russia in 1904! Nothing could speak higher of Japanese craftsmanship than a twice re-tooled 300 year old barrel using modern gunpowder that still continued to function admirably. Such was the effectiveness of the Japanese models, that armorers would display a "proof mark" on their suits of armor by firing an arquebus at the armor at close range, the dent left by the ball proving the ability of the armor to withstand a firearm.

Japanese skill with the arquebus did not stop with design and construction, as they also developed highly effective training manuals for its use in war. In 1560 the arquebus had its debut in a large scale battle and from that point on became a regular feature in samurai warfare. The idea of such a weapon, however, began to have an adverse affect on military leaders. Many regarded the arquebus both as an unwanted invasion of western culture—something Japan had vehemently withstood for centuries—as well as dishonorable for use by dedicated warriors such as the upper class samurai. The arquebus threatened not only the social status quo, but

also the manner in which the samurai tradition-
ally conducted warfare. Matters came to a grave
head after the battle of Nagashino in 1575,
where peasant soldiers armed with the arquebus
slaughtered some of the finest samurai cavalry
in history with rotating volley fire. At the battle
of Komaki, fought in 1584, both of the opposing
commanders had a high percentage of arquebusiers in their ranks and the results of Nagashino
uppermost in their minds. The battle was like
nothing seen before in Japan as both sides,
refusing to attack, dug trenches and waited for
the other to make a move. The result was an
impasse, with both sides firing an occasional
volley or blowing up a land mine, but with no
traditional tactics or maneuvers being employed.
In "Giving Up the Gun: Japan's Reversion to the
Sword, 1543–1879," -one of the only English
texts on this subject—Noel Perrin stated, "In
some ways it (Komaki) was like a scene from
World War I, three and a half centuries ahead
of schedule."

The consequence was that military leaders
began to call for a regulation of firearms, the
specific purpose of which was to deny their use
to the peasants out of a fear of social rebellion.

The armies could keep their guns, of course, but the weapon had to be taken away from civilians. Around 1587 the regent of Japan, Lord Hideyoshi, began the first, albeit surreptitious, step toward gun control. Declaring that he was going to build a magnificent statue of Buddha which was to be fashioned of wood and braced with iron bands, Hideyoshi required all civilians to contribute both their guns and swords toward the construction. Although gun production continued to rise for another two decades, the ground work for gun disarmament had been laid. The next step was centralization of firearm manufacture under government control. This was initiated in 1607 by Lord Tokugawa Ieyasu. As the gunsmiths could now only make weapons under approval or order by the government, the number of guns began to drop and many of the gunsmiths, reduced almost to starvation, returned to making swords. By 1625, with the government's monopoly firmly established, the orders for guns was again reduced and by 1673 less than 400 guns were being made every two years. In 1703, this number was reduced to only 35 large guns in even numbered years and 250 small guns in odd years. This level was maintained for the next 80 years, with further research and development of guns stopping completely in 1725.

The Shimbara Rebellion in 1637 witnessed the last use of guns in Japan for over two hundred years. When Commodore Perry arrived in Tokyo Bay with the "Great White Fleet" in 1853 to try and force the "opening" of Japan to the western world, he was met by samurai armed with only their traditional weapons—swords, spears and bows. Although there were eight-pound artillery pieces positioned to defend Tokyo harbor, these guns had been made in the 1650's and the Japanese had almost completely forgotten how to fire them.

It was only after the arrival of Perry and the impressive western technology he brought with him that the Japanese once again began to actively use firearms. Unable to reply to the superior technological might of the west, Japan was reluctantly forced to abandon the old ways and adopt the new to insure its continued survival as a nation.

A modern photo of Nagoya Castle

GLOSSARY

AIKIDO	Japanese martial art. "the Way of Harmony with ki." (See *ki*.)
ASHIGARU	Foot soldiers.
BUJUTSU	"Bu," war; "jutsu," art. The art of war.
BUSHIDO	"Bushi," warrior; "do," way. The way of the warrior.
DAIMYO	A samurai landowner and warlord.

Archer   *Spearman*   *Ashigaru*

THE WAYS OF THE SAMURAI

DOJO	"Do," way; "jo," place. Place to study the way: a martial arts school.
GI	Two-piece pajamalike uniform worn to practice martial arts.
HAKAMA	Wide, skirtlike trousers worn by samurai and martial arts students.
HARA-KIRI	Ritual suicide by opening the abdomen.
JUDO	Martial art based on flexibility and wrestling.
JUJITSU	Another style of judo.
KAMIKAZE	"Divine winds." Name taken by Japanese suicide pilots in World War II.
KARATE	Japanese martial art.
KATA	Set sequences of martial arts movements.

Farmers and nobles

KATANA	Long, single-edged sword worn by samurai.
KENDO	A martial art, "the Way of the Sword."
KI	Inner life force or energy.
KIAI	Powerful shout used by martial artists.
KYUDO	A martial art, "the Way of the Bow." Archery.
MON	Clan or family crest.
NAGINATA	A spear with a curved blade.
NINJA	Secretive warriors used by the samurai as spies and assassins.
NINJITSU	The art of the ninja.
RONIN	Masterless samurai.
SAMURAI	Member of the warrior class of Japan.

Cavalryman

SASHIMONO   Flag worn by samurai
                     on the battlefield, bear-
                     ing clan crest, or mon.

SENSEI   Teacher or master, term
                     of respect.

SEPPUKU   Formal name for hara-
                     kiri.

SHINTO   Ancient religion of
                     Japan.

SHOGUN   Military dictator of
                     Japan.

TATAMI   Straw floor mat.

WAKIZASHI   The shorter of two
                     swords worn by
                     samurai. (See *katana.)*

YARI   Spear with a straight
                     blade.

ZEN   Form of the Buddhist
                     religion practiced by
                     many samurai.

RECOMMENDED WEBSITE

Samurai Archives
www.samurai-archives.com

An indepth research site on samurai history with information and illustrations on the samurai and their culture, famous battles, timelines, and links.